Science Books
for Young People

by Carolyn Phelan

Booklist Publications
American Library Association
1996

ISBN 0-8389-7837-1

Table of Contents

Introduction

What makes a good science book? Accuracy, yes, but it's not enough. The best books offer intriguing details about the complexity of our world, without a deluge of facts. They challenge our minds to appreciate a clever leap of imagination that leads to a new idea and to recognize the painstaking experimentation that leads to its proof. They lead us through the intricacies of a particular plant cycle or animal behavior or forest fire or chemical reaction, but leave us with a more profound sense of what's happening all around us and even in us. From an intriguing individual phenomenon, they expand our vision outward to encompass the whole universe.

Increasingly, science books for children are beautiful as well. The overall quality of full-color illustration (usually photography) in these books is exceptionally high. Again, it's not enough. But when the artwork supports a text that has something to say and says it well, then young people see more readily and feel more vividly the connections between the words in the book and the world around them.

The following list reflects the best in children's science books today and those most useful to young people from kindergarten age through the eighth grade. When a book is suggested for kindergarten and the primary grades, the grade indicated does not refer to the child's reading level, but to the child's ability to understand it when read aloud. The list is generally limited to pure science: trees, not logging; plants, not farming; the earth, not Earth Day; animals, not pets; sea otters, not the heroic efforts of conservationists to save sea otters. Not *every* choice is a traditional science book, though. Here and there, you'll find a picture book, a poetry book, a magic book, or even a riddle book, chosen for its originality in presenting scientific content.

For public and school libraries, this bibliography can serve as a signpost to good, up-to-date resources. Elementary and middle school teachers will find the books wonderful to use in the classroom. Home-schoolers and other parents will also find them excellent resources for introducing children to the sciences.

The list is organized by subject. Reference books are included within subject areas and the decision of whether a book belongs in circulation, in reference, or in both is left to the librarian. Books of science experiments appear within subject areas as well, since children should perform science experiments and demonstrations to understand the subject explored, not just to practice the scientific method. Compared with the other science categories, many books of experiments were published, but few were chosen. Too many look dull and sound utilitarian. However, the experiment books on this list succeed in presenting the ideas and the processes of science in a way that appeals to children.

Most of the annotations are based on reviews in *Booklist*, the reviewing journal of the American Library Association. These annotations reflect the expertise of many school and public librarians as well as staff reviewers and editors. The selection of titles reflects my experience as a book reviewer, a children's librarian, and a parent. Published from 1990 to 1995, the books listed here offer many roads to understanding science and make every path inviting to young people.

General Science

Ardley, Neil. 101 Great Science Experiments: A Step-by-Step Guide. 1993. illus. Dorling Kindersley, $16.95 (1-56458-404-6).

Gr. 3–5. Many of these 101 science experiments can be found elsewhere, but the book's clean, simple format and clear instructions give it an edge. The activities are grouped into 11 categories, including water and liquids, electricity, motion and machines, and the senses. Most of the experiments are laid out in seven steps or less, with crisp, color photographs and concise captions that make each step easy to follow.

Bibilisco, Stan. The Concise Illustrated Dictionary of Science and Technology. 1993. illus. TAB, $36.95 (0-8306-4152-1); paper, $24.95 (0-8306-4153-X).

Gr. 6–12. An excellent science dictionary for junior and senior high school students, this includes easy-to-follow definitions of common terms from astronomy, chemistry, geology, engineering, biology, mathematics, and physics as well as a few biographical entries.

Busch, Phyllis S. Backyard Safaris: 52 Year-Round Science Adventures. 1995. illus. Simon & Schuster, $16 (0-689-80302-8).

Gr. 4–6. From viewing clouds to feeding chipmunks, this guide suggests science activities for every week of the year.

Cobb, Vikki. Natural Wonders: Stories Science Photos Tell. 1990. illus. Lothrop, $14.95 (0-688-09317-5); lib. ed., $14.88 (0-688-09318-3).

Gr. 4–8. Cobb juxtaposes a large and striking photo with a lucid page of text explaining the scientific phenomenon portrayed. Subjects include a raindrop falling in a pond, the crystalline structure of a diamond, the earth's atmosphere, protozoa in a drop of water, and an insect's view of a flower.

The Dorling Kindersley Science Encyclopedia. 1993. illus. Dorling Kindersley, $39.95 (1-56458-328-7).

Gr. 5–8. Colorful photos and art appear on every page of this thematically arranged science resource. The 400 major entries, generally one to two pages long, includes articles on topics such as kinetic theory, polymers, and tornadoes, as well as biographical sketches of scientists and inventors.

Gallant, Roy A. A Young Person's Guide to Science: Ideas That Change the World. 1993. illus. Macmillan, $16.95 (0-02-735775-9).

Gr. 5–10. Gallant introduces the scientific method, explains how it works and why it works, then surveys knowledge and debate in a number of fields, including biology, ecology, astronomy, psychology, and physics. Written without jargon and illustrated with photos and diagrams, this book provides a readable overview of current scientific thought.

Gardner, Robert. Famous Experiments You Can Do. 1990. illus. Watts, lib. ed., $12.90 (0-531-10883-X).

Gr. 6–12. Gardner describes early investigations into the problems of science and provides directions for using simple equipment to reproduce 33 classic discoveries.

Gardner, Robert. Robert Gardner's Favorite Science Experiments. 1993. illus. Watts, lib. ed., $12.90 (0-531-11038-9); paper, $6.95 (0-531-15255-3).

Gr. 5–8. This handy how-to manual

contains more than 30 experiments for science fair projects and classroom demonstrations in chemistry, mechanics, biology, astronomy, heat, and electricity. One unusual section features the art and science of estimating.

Graham-Barber, Lynda. Toad or Frog, Swamp or Bog? 1994. illus. Four Winds, $15.95 (0-02-736931-5).
Gr. 1–4. This intriguing book explains the differences between animals and natural phenomena that are often confused, such as raven and crow, butterfly and moth, and dolphin and porpoise. Vivid, double-page paintings show the often-confused pairs in their natural setting, while the next spread offers detailed information that clarifies the differences between the two.

Grand, Gail L. Student Science Opportunities. 1994. Wiley, paper $14.95 (0-471-31088-3).
Gr. 6–12. Students who want to pursue scientific interests during the summer will find this an invaluable guide to programs offered throughout the U.S. as well as science competitions during the school year, scholarship opportunities, resources available to women and minorities, and national agencies that sponsor science programs.

Hoban, Tana. Animal, Vegetable, or Mineral. 1995. illus. Greenwillow, $15 (0-688-12747-9).
K–Gr.2. Hoban challenges children to look at the bright, clear photographs and decide whether the things they see are animal, vegetable, or mineral. Some of the photos show something from only one category; others combine all three.

Kingfisher Science Encyclopedia. Ed. by Catherine Headlam. 1993. charts. illus. Kingfisher, $39.95 (1-85697-842-7).
Gr. 3–6. This alphabetically arranged resource includes nearly 1,000 entries

ranging in length from a paragraph to several pages as well as 2,000 color illustrations.

Lang, Susan. Nature in Your Backyard: Simple Activities for Children. 1995. illus. Millbrook, lib. ed., $16.90 (1-56294-451-7).
Gr. 2–4. This practical book offers easy science activities using common household products and natural materials found in the backyard. Each project includes a materials list, simple directions, watercolor illustrations, some thought-provoking questions, and a short explanation of anticipated results.

Macmillan Encyclopedia of Science. 12v. 1991. illus. Macmillan, $360 (0-02-941346-X).
Gr. 4–9. This 12-volume encyclopedia presents 6- to 12-page articles on topics in science and technology as well as capsule biographies of important scientists and inventors. Color photographs, computer-generated images, and well-captioned diagrams are an integral part of each volume.

Markle, Sandra. Science to the Rescue. 1994. illus. Atheneum, $15.95 (0-689-31783-2).
Gr. 4–7. Markle identifies eight problem areas facing people and shows how science has provided a solution. She then challenges readers to build models or make plans to find their own solutions to the problems.

Markle, Sandra. The Young Scientists Guide to Successful Science Projects. 1990. illus. Lothrop, lib. ed., $12.93 (0-688-07217-8); paper, $6.95 (0-688-09137-7).
Gr. 4–9. Markle explains what an experiment is and how to design, perform, interpret, and display it. She covers issues from choosing the topic to controlling variables to answering a sci-

ence fair judge's questions, as she gradually nudges readers into understanding the how and why of the scientific method.

Murray, Peter. Silly Science Tricks (with Professor Solomon Snickerdoodle). 1993. illus. Child's World; dist. by Encyclopaedia Britannica, lib. ed., $14.95 (0-89565-976-X).

Gr. 2–4. Professor Solomon Snickerdoodle, actually a boy in disguise, and his eager aardvark pupil present seven science tricks, including how to make invisible ink, how to blow up a balloon without blowing into it, and how to make a chicken bone pliable enough to tie into a knot.

New Book of Popular Science. 6v. 1994. illus. Grolier, $229 (0-7172-1219-X).

Gr. 5–10. Each book in this dependable six-volume set covers one or two broad topics, such as biology, earth science, and mathematics. Full-color photos and diagrams illustrate informative articles, which are updated in each edition to reflect new discoveries and changing theories in the sciences.

Nye, Bill. Bill Nye the Science Guy's Big Blast of Science. 1993. illus. Addison-Wesley, paper, $12.45 (0-201-60864-2).

Gr. 5–8. In a breezy, informative manner, Nye conducts readers on a whirlwind tour of science, including subjects such as the scientific method, matter, fundamental forces, heat, light, electricity, magnetism, waves, weather, and space. Zippy black-and-white drawings and occasionally zany photographs of the author give the pages an informal look. Nye, Emmy Award–winning host of *Disney Presents Bill Nye, the Science Guy,* communicates in such an accessible style that learning is only a little more labor intensive than listening.

Nye, Bill and **Saunders, Ian**. Bill Nye the Science Guy's Consider the Following: A Way Cool Set of Science Questions, Answers, and Ideas to Ponder. 1995. illus. Disney; dist. by Little, Brown, lib. ed., $13.89 (0-7868-5035-3); paper, $9.95 (0-7868-4054-4).

Gr. 4–7. Each four-page section asks a science question and leads into a discussion of important terms and principles related to one of several science disciplines (biology, geology, physics, etc.) and an easy-to-perform experiment. Nye's conversational tone and his dedication to fitting science into everyday experience make his book a welcome change of pace.

Penrose, Gordon. More Science Surprises from Dr. Zed. 1992. illus. Simon & Schuster, lib. ed., $12 (0-671-77810-2); paper, $6 (0-671-77811-0).

Gr. 1–3. From a colorful series, this large-format book features 13 double-page spreads, each with one or two simple activities, a small, cartoonish drawing of Dr. Zed (a character from OWL/TV), and a large, full-color photograph of a child demonstrating the project.

The Raintree Illustrated Science Encyclopedia. 3d ed. 18v. 1991. illus. Steck-Vaughn/Raintree, $470 (0-8172-3800-X).

Gr. 3–7. A British import well adapted for American use, this encyclopedia covers a broad range of topics, including mathematics, psychology, geography, science projects, and biographies of famous scientists. Written by university-affiliated subject consultants and illustrated in full color, this attractive set serves as a useful resource for elementary and middle school students.

Science and Technology. 1993. illus. Oxford, $30 (0-19-910143-4).

Gr. 4–7. Each entry in this book provides two or three pages of information with a fact panel for quick reference.

The book is divided into five sections: science and materials, space, energy and the home, transport technology, and information technology.

Simon, Seymour. Science Dictionary. 1994. illus. HarperCollins, $29.95 (0-06-025630-3); lib. ed., $29.89 (0-06-025630-3).

Gr. 4–8. Simon states that "like any foreign language, science can be translated into ideas and concepts that use simple English words." He does a fine job of translation in this illustrated science dictionary, with more than 2,000 up-to-date entries covering all branches of science.

Smith, Norman F. How to Do Successful Science Projects. Rev. ed. 1990. illus. Messner, lib. ed., $11.98 (0-671-70685-3); paper, $5.95 (0-671-70686-1).

Gr. 5–8. Encouraging students to undertake investigative science projects rather than displays or demonstrations, Smith provides a guidebook to every phase of the process.

Take Me to Your Liter: Science and Math Jokes. Ed. by Charles Keller. 1991. illus. Pippin, lib. ed., $13.95 (0-945912-13-7).

Gr. 3–6. "Question: What did one geologist say to the other? Answer: Are you going to the rock festival?" More groans than giggles here, but idiotic riddles are great for defusing tension, especially where there's a fear of math and science.

White, Laurence B. and **Broekel, Ray.** Illus. by **Seltzer, Meyer.** Shazam! Simple Science Magic. 1991. Albert Whitman, $11.95 (0-8075-7332-9).

Gr. 3–6. This entertaining book shows young magicians how to perform 20 mystifying tricks and how to understand the science underlying the magic. Who could resist a chapter entitled "How to Hypnotize a Potato"? The informal tone of the writing and illustrations creates a playful approach, but the science is solid and well explained.

Wilkes, Angela. My First Science Book. 1990. illus. Knopf, $13 (0-679-80583-4); lib. ed., $13.99 (0-679-90583-9).

K–Gr.4. This large-format book takes a step-by-step approach to simple projects, such as demonstrating static electricity with balloons, experimenting with magnets, doing litmus tests using common foods, and making a fingerprint kit, a paper airplane, and shadow puppets. Small, colorful photos accompany the clear instructions.

Wollard, Kathy. How Come? 1993. illus. Workman, paper, $10.95 (1-56305-324-1).

Gr. 5–9. Why is the sky blue? Do parrots understand what they say? Drawn from Wollard's syndicated newspaper column, these and other questions are answered in considerable detail, in understandable terms, and in ways that relate to young people's everyday experiences.

Astronomy

Apfel, Necia H. Orion, the Hunter. 1995. illus. Clarion, $16.95 (0-395-68962-7).

Gr. 3–6. The constellation Orion provides ample material for discussing astronomy since it includes the Orion nebula, the Horsehead nebula, the red supergiant star Betelgeuse, and the blue-white giant star Rigel. Spectacular photographs, supplemented by diagrams, illustrate this fine book.

Apfel, Necia. Voyager to the Planets. 1991. illus. Clarion, $15.45 (0-395-55209-5); paper, $6.95 (0-395-60522-4).

Gr. 3–5. A special alignment of the planets allowed a single spacecraft to fly past Jupiter, Saturn, Uranus, and Neptune. Apfel follows *Voyager 2's* grand tour and presents data and photographs gathered from its mission.

Asimov, Isaac. How Did We Find Out about Pluto? 1991. illus. Walker, $12.95 (0-8027-6991-9); lib. ed., $13.85 (0-8027-6992-6).

Gr. 5–8. Asimov tells how astronomers discovered Pluto and its moon Charon, how they learned about them during a series of eclipses, and why the search continues for a tenth planet beyond Pluto's orbit. Among the books in this series is *How Did We Find Out about Neptune?*

Branley, Franklyn. The Big Dipper. Rev. ed. illus. HarperCollins, $13.95 (0-06-020511-3); paper, $4.95 (0-06-445100-3).

K–Gr.5. Written and illustrated with simplicity and directness, this appealing picture book introduces children to a familiar constellation in the night sky.

Branley, Franklyn. Venus: Magellan Explores Our Twin Planet. 1994. illus. HarperCollins, $16 (0-06-020298-X).

Gr. 3–6. Beginning with *Magellan's* launching in 1989, Branley briefly explains the space probe's mission and offers a lucid description of Venus' motions, features, makeup, structure, and significant similarities to Earth. Diagrams and photos, most in full color, illustrate the text.

Burrows, William E. Mission to Deep Space: Voyagers' Journey of Discovery. 1993. illus. W. H. Freeman, $17.95 (0-7167-6500-4).

Gr. 4–6. One among many books presenting the *Voyager* missions to explore the solar system, this discusses the spacecraft, the messages from Earth they carried, and what was known about a planet before and after they flew past. The writing excels at conveying the excitement felt by those involved in the missions as the encounters took place.

Cole, Joanna. The Magic School Bus, Lost in the Solar System. 1990. illus. Scholastic, $14.95 (0-590-41428-3); paper, $3.95 (0-590-41429-1).

K–Gr.4. Setting out on a field trip to the planetarium, the students in wacky Ms. Frizzle's class end up in space for a quick tour of the solar neighborhood. With lively illustrations and a text that interweaves information with comic narrative, this book entertains while it teaches about the solar system.

Couper, Heather and **Henbest, Nigel.** How the Universe Works. 1994. illus. Reader's Digest; dist. by Random, $25 (0-89577-576-X).

Gr. 4–6. Each double-page spread in

this large-format book highlights one subject with a brief introductory text, at least one activity, and sometimes a boxed sidelight. Bright, clear photographs against a white background add great visual appeal.

Couper, Heather and **Henbest, Nigel.** The Space Atlas. 1992. illus. Harcourt/ Gulliver, $16.95 (0-15-200598-6).

Gr. 3–6. Fully illustrated with colorful paintings and photographs, this large-format atlas includes descriptions of planets, explanations of phenomena, boxes including suggested activities ("Make a Simple Sundial"), and tables displaying facts such as the distance, luminosity, and types of stars and galaxies.

Fisher, Leonard Everett. Galileo. 1992. illus. Macmillan, $15.95 (0-02-735235-8).

Gr. 3–8. The concise, straightforward narrative depicts Galileo as a brilliant and contentious astronomer, mathematician, and physicist whose dedication to scientific truth incurred the wrath of his fellow scientists and the Roman Catholic Church. The sophisticated look of the artwork, coupled with a fact-filled text, makes the book attractive to readers and science students considerably older than picture-book age.

Fowler, Allan. So That's How the Moon Changes Shape! 1991. illus. Childrens Press, $10.75 (0-516-04917-8); paper, $3.95 (0-516-44917-6).

K–Gr. 2. Colorful photographs illustrate the very simple, short text explaining the waxing and waning of the moon. The vocabulary and the large, clear type make the book appropriate for beginning readers. Also from the Rookie Reader series are Fowler's The Sun Is Always Shining Somewhere and The Sun's Family of Planets.

Fradin, Dennis B. Mercury. 1990. illus. Childrens Press, lib. ed., $12.85 (0-516-01186-3); paper, $4.95 (0-516-41186-1).

Gr. 2–4. With large print, generous space between the lines, and many full-color illustrations, this New True Book describes the discovery, physical features, and mysteries of the planet Mercury. Other books in the series include Fradin's Jupiter, Saturn, Uranus, Neptune, and Pluto.

Gardner, Robert. Space. 1994. illus. Twenty-First Century, lib. ed., $16.95 (0-8050-2851-X).

Gr. 6–9. Colorful pictures and diagrams illustrate the informative text and many simple activities related to space science. Topics include weightlessness, gravity, and how people discovered the shape of the earth and its movement in relation to the sun.

George, Michael. The Sun. 1991. illus. Creative Education; dist. by Encyclopaedia Britannica, $18.95 (0-88682-402-8).

Gr. 3–8. Stunning full-color photographs illustrate this presentation of the sun's structure, activity, future, and effect on the earth. Michael's Stars is another book in this visually dynamic series.

Gibbons, Gail. Stargazers. 1992. illus. Holiday, $15.95 (0-8234-0983-X).

K–Gr.3. In the brightly colored illustrations, a family observes the night sky; in the text, Gibbons briefly introduces stars, the Milky Way, constellations, telescopes, and planetariums. Similar in format, her book The Planets surveys the solar system.

Gustafson, John. Stars, Clusters, and Galaxies. 1992. illus. Messner, $12.98 (0-671-72536-X); paper, $6.95 (0-671-72537-8).

Gr. 3–7. Combining activities with

information, this illustrated guidebook explains stars, galaxies, and nebulae. Gustafson encourages readers to observe them firsthand, offering tips for viewing the night sky with or without telescopes and binoculars. Look for the companion volume, *Planets, Moons, and Meteors.*

Harris, Alan and **Weissman, Paul**. The Great Voyager Adventure. 1990. illus. Messner, $14.95 (0-671-72539-4).

Gr. 4–8. Packed with information, diagrams, charts, and photographs, this well-written book has an informal style and the useful feature of explaining out-of-this-world facts in down-to-earth terms.

Hirst, Robin. My Place in Space. 1990. illus. Orchard, $13.95 (0-531-0589-X); paper, $5.95 (0-531-07030-1).

K–Gr.1. When an obnoxious, loud-mouthed bus driver asks Henry and Rosie if they know where they live, he gets a precise answer: "12 Main Street, Gumbridge, Australia, Southern Hemisphere . . . Earth . . . solar system . . . solar neighborhood . . . Milky Way . . . Virgo supercluster . . . the universe."

Kelch, Joseph. Small Worlds: Exploring the 60 Moons of Our Solar System. 1990. illus. Messner, $13.95 (0-671-70014-6); lib. ed., $16.98 (0-671-70013-8).

Gr. 5–8. This book takes readers on a guided tour to each moon of the solar system, offers a concise history of space exploration, and discusses the possibility of space colonization.

Kerrod, Robin. The Children's Space Atlas: A Voyage of Discovery for Young Astronauts. 1992. illus. Millbrook, $16.95 (1-56294-164-X); lib. ed., $16.95 (1-56294-721-4); paper, $10.95 (0-685-72514-6).

Gr. 2–6. Beautifully illustrated, this oversize atlas includes historical facts as well as maps of the night skies and information about the planets and other topics in astronomy.

Kraske, Robert. Asteroids: Invaders from Space. 1995. illus. Simon & Schuster/Atheneum, $15 (0-689-31860-X).

Gr. 5–7. Kraske combines dramatic stories of cosmic collisions with solid astronomy and earth science in this discussion of asteroids.

Krupp, E. C. The Moon and You. 1993. illus. Macmillan, $13.95 (0-02-751142-1).

Gr. 3–6. "In a baseball game on the moon, every hit would be a home run. The game would never be called on account of rain. With no air to carry the sound, you could never hear the fans cheer." Set in a picture-book format, the straightforward, conversational text briefly explains the history, geography, orbit, phases, eclipses, gravity, and exploration of the moon.

Lauber, Patricia. How We Learned the World Is Round. 1990. illus. HarperCollins/Crowell, $14 (0-690-04860-2); lib. ed., $13.89 (0-690-04862-9); paper, $4.50 (0-06-445109-7).

K–Gr.3. Lauber explains in simple language that although the earth appears flat, the ancient Greeks deduced its spherical shape from their observations of ships and solar eclipses.

Lauber, Patricia. Journey to the Planets. 4th ed. 1993. illus. Crown, $20 (0-517-59029-8); paper, $9.95 (0-531-07057-3).

Gr. 4–8. Full-color photographs, mainly from NASA, brighten the pages of this well-written guide to the solar system.

Lauber, Patricia. Seeing Earth from Space. 1990. illus. Orchard, $20 (0-531-05902-2).

Gr. 4–8. For a new perspective on the

home planet, take a look at NASA's space-based, full-color photographs of Earth. Lauber explains the often other-worldly scenes and ends with a moving statement of how "seeing Earth from space" has changed our thinking over the last few decades.

Leedy, Loren. Postcards from Pluto. 1993. Holiday, $15.95 (0-8234-1000-5).

K–Gr.2. Illustrated with acrylic paintings, this picture book features post-cards sent home by a group of children touring the planets with an informative robot for their guide. Young children will find this an appealing trip through the solar system.

Levitt, I. M. and **Marshall, Roy K.** Star Maps for Beginners. Rev. ed. 1992. Simon and Schuster/Fireside $10 (0-671-79187-7).

Gr. 4–10. Ilustrated with star charts for each month, this reliable guide includes the history of the constellations and the stories behind them, the locations of the planets in the sky through 1997, and what to look for in the night sky every month of the year.

McTavish, Douglas. Galileo. 1991. illus. Bookwright; dist. by Watts, lib. ed., $12.40 (0-531-18405-6).

Gr. 4–8. Illustrated with period prints and full-color artwork, this succinct, lively biography describes the life and scientific contributions of Galileo.

Our Satellite: The Moon. 1994. illus. Barron's, $12.95 (0-8120-6369-4); paper, $6.95 (0-8120-1740-4).

Gr. 3–6. Succinct writing and large, full-color paintings make this a good resource for children studying the moon. Each two-page spread concerns a single subject, such as "Observing a Lunar Eclipse" or "The Far Side of the Moon." Other books in the Window on

the Universe include *Galaxies* and *Our Planet: Earth.*

Pinkney, Andrea Davis. Illus. by **Pinkney, Brian**. Dear Benjamin Banneker. 1994. Harcourt, $14.95 (0-15-200417-3).

Gr.2–4. This picture biography tells of Benjamin Banneker, who was born to free black parents in 1731, taught himself astronomy, and wrote an almanac. Distinctive artwork, using subtle shades of oil paints over scratchboard pictures, illustrates this handsome book.

Ride, Sally and **O'Shaughnessy, Tam**. The Third Planet: Exploring the Earth from Space. 1994. illus. Crown, $15 (0-517-5936-0); lib. ed., $15.99 (0-517-59362-9).

Gr. 4–7. One of the few to see the home planet from space, Sally Ride brings a unique perspective to the discussion of Earth's land features, oceans, atmosphere, and fragile biosphere. The dramatic format features clear, full-color photos and diagrams that seem to light up against the glossy black pages.

Ride, Sally. Voyager: An Adventure to the Edge of the Solar System. 1992. illus. Crown, $14.99 (0-517-58157-4); lib. ed., $14.99 (0-517-58158-2).

Gr. 3–8. In a book illustrated with splendid, full-color photographs from NASA, astronaut Sally Ride describes the technology and discoveries of the *Voyager* missions, focusing on how they expanded our knowledge of the solar system.

Ridpath, Ian. The Facts On File Atlas of Stars and Planets: A Beginner's Guide to the Universe. 1993. illus. Facts On File, $16.95 (0-8160-2926-1).

Gr. 4–8. Illustrated with full-color photos, paintings, and diagrams, this large-format volume includes information on the sun, planets, stars, comets, asteroids, meteorites, and galaxies, as well as binoculars and telescopes. The clear presentation makes this a good choice for basic research.

Robinson, Fay. Space Probes to the Planets. 1993. illus. Albert Whitman, lib. ed., $14.95 (0-8075-7548-8).

Gr. 2–4. Stunning color photographs and diagrams illustrate this compact volume, which begins with the Mercury project and continues through our solar system planet by planet, discussing space probes and their contribution to our knowledge of astronomy.

Ronan, Colin A. The Universe Explained: The Earth-Dwellers Guide to the Mysteries of Space. 1994. illus. Holt, $35 (0-8050-3488-9).

Gr. 4–8. This attractive book is a treasury of information illustrated with excellent, colorful photographs and diagrams. Turning to everyday objects and events to explain more complex phenomena, the author clearly expresses knowledge and theories about planets, stars, nebulae, galaxies, and the universe.

Rosen, Sidney. Which Way to the Milky Way? 1992. illus. Carolrhoda, lib. ed., $19.95 (0-87614-709-0).

Gr. 2–5. Rosen provides a step-by-step trip through the galaxy, featuring cartoon characters who ask questions like, "What is the Milky Way, anyway?" and "What does the Milky Way have to do with us on Earth?" Other titles in this user-friendly series include Can You Find a Planet? How Far Is a Star? and Where Does the Moon Go?

Schaaf, Fred. The Amateur Astronomer: Explorations and Investigations. 1994. illus. Watts, lib. ed., $12.90 (0-531-11138-5).

Gr. 6–10. For readers who want to pursue astronomy on their own, Schaaf offers practical advice on choosing a telescope and good ideas for observing meteor showers, eclipses of the moon, and other phenomena.

Schloss, Muriel. Venus. 1991. illus. Watts, lib. ed., $12.90 (0-531-20019-1).

Gr. 3–6. Many well-captioned photographs, drawings, and paintings illustrate this attractive and informative introduction to Venus. Other astronomy books in the First Book series include Daily's The Sun, Mercury, Earth, and Pluto; Landau's Mars, Jupiter, Saturn, and Neptune; and Shepherd's Uranus.

Simon, Seymour. Mercury. 1992. illus. Morrow, $14 (0-688-10544-0); lib. ed., $13.93 (0-688-10545-9).

Gr. 3–5. Using the same eye-catching design as in his other books on space, Simon describes the planet Mercury. The large, full-color photos and clearly written text continue to draw readers to this these appealing books, which include Venus, Neptune, Our Solar System, and Comets, Meteors, and Asteroids.

Simon, Seymour. Space Words: A Dictionary. 1991. illus. HarperCollins, $15 (0-06-022532-7); lib. ed., $14.89 (0-06-022533-5).

Gr. 1–3. This illustrated dictionary discusses terms used in describing outer space, beginning with Apollo Program and ending with Zodiac.

Stannard, Russell. Our Universe: A Guide to What's Out There. 1995. illus. Kingfisher, $14.95 (1-85697-551-7).

Gr. 5–8. Stannard brings a conversational tone to his guided tour of the universe. Whether discussing subatomic particles, the Big Bang, the planets, or supernovae, the writing conveys his enthusiasm as well as his clear thinking. Full-color artwork brightens the pages of this appealing book.

Star Walk. Ed. by Seymour Simon. 1995. illus. Morrow, $15 (0-688-11887-9); lib. ed., $14.93 (0-688-11887-7).

Gr. 4–8. This unusual book combines stunning photography with thought-provoking poems about stars and space.

Vogt, Gregory. Magellan and the Radar Mapping of Venus. 1992. illus. Millbrook, lib. ed., $15.90 (1-56294-146-1).

Gr. 5–8. Vogt describes the *Magellan* space probe that enabled astronomers to map the surface of Venus in remarkable detail. Also in the Missions in Space series is Vogt's *The Hubble Space Telescope.*

Vogt, Gregory L. Pluto. 1994. illus. Millbrook, lib. ed., $12.90 (1-56294-393-6).

Gr. 2–5. Amply illustrated with photos, diagrams, and paintings of scenes in space, this book presents basic information about the planet's discovery, its characteristics, and the questions Pluto raises for astronomers. Vogt's series on the planets includes *Mercury, Venus, Mars, Neptune,* and *Uranus.*

Vogt, Gregory L. The Solar System: Facts and Exploration. 1995. illus. Twenty-First Century, lib. ed., $18.98 (0-8050-3249-5).

Gr. 5–8. A lively, concise guide to the planets, moons, asteroids, comets, and meteoroids, this book also includes accounts of discoveries and disappointments in the space program, giving readers a feel for the ongoing challenge of understanding the solar system. The excellent full-color illustrations include many recent images from the Hubble space telescope.

Time and Seasons

Branley, Franklin M. Keeping Time: From the Beginning and into the 21st Century. 1993. illus. Houghton, $13.95 (0-395-47777-8).

Gr. 4–6. From the history of time-keeping and calendars to the theory of relativity to the reasons we divide time as we do, Branley challenges readers with difficult, abstract concepts and offers simple, concrete projects. The book presents a great deal of information in clear and readable form, while cartoonlike ink drawings provide an upbeat counterpoint to the text.

Gibbons, Gail. The Reasons for Seasons. 1995. illus. Holiday, $15.95 (0-8234-1174-5).

K–Gr. 3. Gibbons uses simple words and clear, colorful pictures to explain the seasons, solstices, and equinoxes. Besides discussing the earth's tilt and orbit, she also comments on what people and animals do in each season of the year.

Hirschi, Ron. Fall. 1991. illus. Dutton/Cobblehill, $14 (0-525-65053-9).

K–Gr.2. Hirschi and photographer Mangelsen portray the seasons as they come to meadow, woodland, and tundra, rather than city, suburb, and barnyard. As in Spring, Summer, and Winter, the crisp full-color photos are laid out on broad white pages and accompanied by a brief text in large print.

Leslie, Clare Walker. Nature All Year Long. 1991. illus. Greenwillow, $16.95 (0-688-09183-0).

Gr. 1–5. For backyard naturalists as well as school classes, this inviting book presents each month in terms of the plant and animal life dwelling in a particular habitat during that time of the year.

Llewellyn, Claire. My First Book of Time. 1992. illus. Dorling Kindersley, $14.95 (1-879431-78-5).

K–Gr.2. With clear explanations, simple experiments, and full-color photographs, this oversize volume introduces children to the abstract and sometimes elusive concept of time. Scattered throughout, pictures of little yellow clocks indicate that readers can open up the foldout clock at the back of the book to solve a puzzle.

Markle, Sandra. Exploring Autumn: A Season of Science Activities, Puzzlers, and Games. 1991. illus. Atheneum, $14.95 (0-689-31620-8).

Gr. 4–7. In a chatty companion to her other books on the seasons, Markle combines science, history, myth, anecdotes, festival activities, and quizzes. Though there's lots of information, the style is never dry and Markle isn't afraid to be lyrical or silly from time to time.

Ryder, Joanne. Illus. by **Nolan, Dennis.** Under Your Feet. 1990. Four Winds, $14.95 (0-02-777955-6).

K–Gr.2. Following a boy through the seasons, this book tells of the animals beneath his feet: moles race along their tunnels, fish dart through the lake as he swims, and worms huddle in deep winter burrows. Watercolor paintings feature occasional cutaway illustrations showing the seasonal landscape above and the action below ground level.

Simon, Seymour. Winter across America. 1994. illus. Hyperion; dist. by Little, Brown, $14.95 (0-7868-0019-4); lib. ed., $14.89 (0-7868-2015-2).

Gr. 3–5. The book's focus moves from the Arctic Circle to Alaska to the Baja California coastal waters, then eastward across the continent, as Simon comments on topics such as winter storms and animal migration. Excellent color photographs, often breathtaking scenes of landscapes and animals, appear throughout the book. Other volumes in the series highlight spring, summer, and autumn.

Singer, Marilyn. Nine o'Clock Lullaby. 1991. illus. HarperCollins, lib. ed., $14.89 (0-06-025648-6); paper, $4.95 (0-06-443319-6).

K–Gr.3. As a mother reads a quiet bedtime story to her child (9 p.m. in Brooklyn), readers are transported around the world to view a series of 16 simultaneous happenings on six continents. With vibrant naive paintings complementing the rhythmic text, this makes a good, simple introduction to the concept of time zones.

Physics and Chemistry

Ardley, Neil. The Science Book of Sound. 1991. illus. Harcourt/Gulliver, $9.95 (0-15-200579-X).

Gr. 1–3. One of a series of science activity books exploring topics such as light, energy, magnets, electricity, motion, and gravity, this volume features a hands-on approach to the physics of sound. Colorful photographs clearly show the simple equipment needed and the steps to be taken.

Bell, J. L. Soap Science: A Science Book Bubbling with 36 Experiments. 1993. illus. Addison-Wesley, paper, $9.57 (0-201-62451-6).

Gr. 3–6. With appealing ink-and-watercolor illustrations on every page, this paperback combines good science with good fun. From discussing the composition of soap to making a bubble fountain or thermometer, it's varied in content, upbeat in tone, and informative every step of the way.

Billings, Charlene W. Superconductivity: From Discovery to Breakthrough. 1991. illus. Dutton/Cobblehill, $15.95 (0-525-65048-2).

Gr. 4–8. Illustrated with many photographs, this book defines superconductivity, explains how it works, and details the research that led to the development of superconductors.

Cobb, Vicki and **Cobb, Josh**. Light Action: Amazing Experiments with Optics. 1993. illus. HarperCollins, $15 (0-06-021436-8); lib. ed., $14.89 (0-06-021437-6).

Gr. 5–8. Cobb presents information about optics and explores its basic principles through well-designed activities. Cheerful line drawings and diagrams illustrate the text.

Cobb, Vicki. Why Doesn't the Sun Burn Out? and Other Not Such Dumb Questions about Energy. 1990. illus. Dutton/Lodestar, $13.95 (0-525-67301-6).

Gr. 2–5. Posing nine questions concerning force and energy, Cobb discusses stored, kinetic, heat, light, and chemical energy, as well as radioactivity and Einstein's theory of relativity. Like her other Dumb Questions books (on matter and motion), this is illustrated with line drawings and diagrams.

Dorros, Arthur. Me and My Shadow. 1990. illus. Scholastic, paper, $12.95 (0-590-42772-5).

Gr. 1–3. With colorful artwork and simple wording, this picture book introduces the concept of shadows. From the shadows of children on the playground to the shadow of the moon during a solar eclipse, Dorros discusses and illustrates the subject in an appealing, child-like way.

Fisher, Leonard Everett. Marie Curie. 1994. illus. Macmillan, $14.95 (0-02-735375-3).

Gr. 3–6. Fisher describes Curie's childhood, education, work, illness, and honors through acrylic paintings and a clearly written text. This dramatic, large-format volume is more memorable than many lengthier science biographies.

Friedhoffer, Robert. Matter and Energy. 1992. illus. Watts, lib. ed., $13.40 (0-531-11051-6).

Gr. 6–8. One of six volumes in the Scientific Magic series, this book draws on Friedhoffer's experience as a professional magician to present tricks and experiments that can be used to explain scientific principles and to surprise an audience. Here he examines topics such as inertia, energy, and the three states of matter in a highly entertaining manner. Illustrations include photographs and amusing line drawings.

Gardner, Robert. Electricity and Magnetism. 1994. illus. Twenty-First Century, lib. ed., $16.95 (0-8050-2850-1).
Gr. 6–9. Gardner discusses magnets and magnetic fields, simple electric charges, the development of the electromagnet and electric motor, and the future of electric power. Full-color pictures and diagrams illustrate the series of activities that follows each discussion, leading readers into a fuller understanding of the subject.

Gardner, Robert. Science Projects about Chemistry. 1994. illus. Enslow, lib. ed., $17.95 (0-89490-531-7).
Gr. 6–9. Whether he's describing how to build a volcano or make a fire extinguisher, Gardner manages to convey the fun of learning chemistry. In this entry from the Science Projects series, which includes topics such as light, heat, and electricity, he carefully spells out the materials needed, notes precautions, and describes probable results for each project.

Gherman, Beverly. The Mysterious Rays of Dr. Rontgen. 1994. illus. Atheneum, $14.95 (0-689-31839-1).
Gr. 2–5. A picture-book biography of the man who discovered X rays combines the excitement of scientific discovery with an accessible explanation of how the rays work. Handsome oil paintings on every page help to personalize the drama, but the focus is on the research, painstaking as well as brilliant.

Lauber, Patricia. What Do You See & How Do You See It? 1994. Crown, $17 (0-517-59390-4); lib. ed., $17.99 (0-516-59391-2).
Gr. 3–6. Excellent full-color photographs and diagrams illustrate Lauber's clear discussion of light, lenses, colors, the eye, and the infrared.

Skurzynski, Gloria. Zero Gravity. 1994. illus. Bradbury, $14.95 (0-02-782925-1).
Gr. 2–4. Skurzynski discusses the sensation of zero gravity in orbiting space shuttles, explaining it in terms of physical forces, and then describes astronauts' experiences of weightlessness while orbiting the earth. Full-color illustrations appear throughout the book, including many intriguing photographs of astronauts working aboard the space shuttles.

Souza, D. M. Northern Lights. 1994. illus. Carolrhoda, $17.50 (0-87614-799-6); paper, $7.95 (0-87614-799-6).
Gr. 5–7. Using a photo-essay format, with pictures of skies in dazzling light and color, Souza introduces the Northern Lights and the physics that lies behind their mysterious beauty.

Stwertka, Albert. The World of Atoms and Quarks. 1995. illus. Twenty-First Century, $18.98 (0-8050-3533-8).
Gr. 6–10. Photographs and full-color diagrams illustrate the history of atomic theory in physics over the past 100 years. Stwertka's explanations are more understandable than most as he tells how scientists have discovered particles and structures too small to be observed.

VanCleave, Janice. Janice VanCleave's Electricity: Mind-Boggling Experiments You Can Turn into Science Fair Projects. 1994. illus. Wiley, paper $9.95 (0-471-31010-7).
Gr. 4–7. VanCleave, a prolific author of science project books, offers 20 experiments with electricity as part of her Spectacular Science Project series, which also includes books on molecules, gravity, and magnets.

Vare, Ethlie Ann. Adventurous Spirit: A Story about Ellen Swallow Richards.

1992. illus. Carolrhoda, lib. ed., $14.95 (0-87614-733-3).

Gr. 3–6. Illustrated with handsome shaded-pencil drawings, this short biography tells of the first woman in America to become a professional chemist. Quotations from Richards' diary and letters enliven this account of her life.

Vecchione, Glen. Magnet Science. 1995. illus. Sterling, $13.95 (0-8069-0888-2).

Gr. 5–8. This clearly written book presents magnetism from ancient Greek legend to the space program. Vecchione introduces hands-on learning about magnets through a variety of activities, from simple (magnetizing a screwdriver) to practical (building a motor), from playful (making a magnetic hockey game) to out-of-this-world (collecting micrometeorites).

Wells, Robert E. Is a Blue Whale the Biggest Thing There Is? 1993. illus. Albert Whitman, $13.95 (0-8075-3655-5); paper, $6.95 (0-8075-3656-3).

Gr. 1–3. In a picture book designed to expand children's horizons, Wells makes the inconceivable more imaginable through original, concrete images: the earth as one of a packet of marbles dwarfed by the sun, or the sun as one orange in a crate that looks insignificant beside Antares. Lively ink-and-watercolor illustrations brighten the pages for small children who are fascinated by big things.

Wells, Robert E. What's Smaller Than a Pygmy Shrew? 1995. illus. Albert Whitman, $13.95 (0-8075-8837-7); paper, $6.95 (0-8075-8838-5).

Gr. 1–3. In a companion book, Wells goes to the opposite extreme when he compares the sizes of various animals right down to a single-cell paramecium. Going beyond the cellular level, he introduces molecules, atoms, electrons, and quarks. Despite the problems inherent in illustrating what cannot even be observed, this picture book succeeds in entertaining and intriguing young children with a relatively sophisticated subject.

Westray, Kathleen. A Color Sampler. 1993. illus. Ticknor & Fields, $14.95 (0-395-65940-X).

Gr. 1–4. Westray introduces pure colors, mixed colors, tints, shades, and complements. Using geometric motifs based on classic quilt patterns, this attractive book features bright, true colors and an intelligent discussion of basic concepts.

Wiese, Jim. Rocket Science: 50 Flying, Floating, Flipping, Spinning Gadgets Kids Create Themselves. 1995. illus. Wiley, paper, $12.95 (0-471-11357-3).

Gr. 3–6. Arranged into six chapters showcasing principles related to physics and chemistry, this book presents appealing experiments that will start kids thinking about how and why things work. Most make use of materials found around the house or in the garage, and diagrams are plentiful and adequately labeled.

Zubrowski, Bernie. Illus. by **Doty, Roy.** Mirrors: Finding Out about the Properties of Light. 1992. Morrow/Boston Children's Museum, $13.95 (0-688-10592-0); paper, $6.95 (0-688-10591-2).

Gr. 4–7. Like the other books in this dependable series, including *Making Waves* and *Shadow Play*, *Mirrors* takes a hands-on approach to science, in this case, the science of light. Zubrowski offers a series of games and activities that really do sound like fun, from the monster maze to the Mylar cylinder reflections, and they *look* like fun in Doty's drawings.

Earth Science

Ardley, Neil. The Science Book of Weather. 1992. illus. Harcourt/Gulliver, $9.95 (0-15-200624-9).

Gr. 1–4. Clear, colorful photographs illustrate simple activities such as making a weather vane, a rain gauge, and a bottle barometer. From the same series, *The Science Book of Water* provides appealing activities exploring the properties of water.

Berger, Melvin and **Berger, Gilda.** Water, Water Everywhere: A Book about the Water Cycle. 1995. illus. Ideals, lib. ed., $12 (1-57102-056-X); paper, $4.50 (1-57102-042-X).

Gr. 2–4. Explaining a complex subject in simple words with lots of well-chosen examples and colorful illustrations, this book explains the water cycle and discusses how water reaches homes, how sewage is treated, and how to save water.

Booth, Basil. Earthquakes and Volcanoes. 1992. illus. Macmillan/New Discovery, lib. ed., $13.95 (0-02-711735-9).

Gr. 5–8. This large-format picture essay explores the interrelationship of earthquakes and volcanoes and dispels some misconceptions—for instance, that extinct volcanoes are dead.

Branley, Franklyn M. Earthquakes. 1990. Harper/Crowell, $15 (0-690-04661-8); lib. ed., $14.89 (0-690-04663-4).

Gr. 1–4. Branley explains earthquakes and how they change the earth. On every page, bright line-and-watercolor pictures illustrate scenes such as shaking cityscapes, concepts such as waves emanating from the epicenter of a quake, and practical advice on what to do when the house begins to jiggle.

Cole, Joanna. The Magic School Bus inside a Hurricane. 1995. illus. Scholastic, $14.95 (0-590-44686-X).

Gr. 1–4. Ms. Frizzle's class boards the Magic School Bus for a trip into the clouds to investigate hurricanes. The brightly colored illustrations, brimming with details, add comic relief and enhance the easy-to-absorb meteorology lessons.

Conley, Andrea. Window on the Deep: The Adventures of Underwater Explorer Sylvia Earle. 1991. illus. Watts, $14.95 (0-531-15232-4); lib. ed., $14.90 (0-531-11119-9).

Gr. 3–6. Beautifully illustrated with full-color photographs, this book describes the explorations of Sylvia Earle, the diver, explorer, and scientist. The well-written narrative celebrates her successes and emphasizes her commitment to learning about ocean life.

DeWitt, Lynda. Illus. by **Croll, Carolyn.** What Will the Weather Be? 1991. HarperCollins, lib. ed., $13.89 (0-06-021597-6); paper, $4.50 (0-06-445113-5).

Ages 5–8. From the Let's-Read-and-Find-Out series, this illustrated introduction to weather forecasting includes meteorological concepts such as fronts, cloud formations, temperature, humidity, and air pressure. Colorful artwork appears throughout the book.

Dorros, Arthur. Follow the Water from Brook to Ocean. 1991. illus. HarperCollins, lib. ed., $14.89 (0-06-021599-2); paper, $4.95 (0-06-445115-1).

K–Gr.3. Also from the dependable Let's-Read-and-Find-Out science series, this picture book describes the earthbound segment of the water cycle, beginning with melting snow on a mountain and following the resulting brook as it flows into a stream, a river, and finally the ocean. Cheerful line-and-watercolor art illustrates the text.

George, Michael. Glaciers. 1991. illus. Creative Education; dist. by Encyclopaedia Britannica, $15.95 (1-56846-061-9); lib. ed., $14.95 (0-88682-401-X).

Gr. 3–8. Dramatic full-color illustrations will draw readers to this book on the formation and types of glaciers and their past, present, and possible future effects on the earth's ecosystem.

George, Michael. Volcanoes. 1991. illus. Creative Education; dist. by Encyclopaedia Britannica, $15.95 (1-56846-065-1); lib. ed., $18.95 (0-88682-403-6).

Gr. 3–8. Captivating in presentation and dramatic in content, this book offers a concise text illustrated by exquisite photos of active and dormant volcanoes, showing how the planet's crust is formed and changed by eruptions of the molten layer beneath the surface.

Gibbons, Gail. Planet Earth, Inside Out. 1995. Morrow, $15 (0-688-09680-8); lib. ed., $14.93 (0-688-09681-6).

Gr. 2–4. Gibbons explains the structure of the earth and its ever-changing surface in simple words illustrated with clear, colorful diagrams, maps, and pictures.

Gibbons, Gail. Weather Words. 1990. illus. Holiday, $15.95 (0-8234-0805-1); paper, $5.95 (0-8234-0952-X).

Gr. 1–4. With fresh colors and a friendly format, this beginning book uses simple words and clear illustrations to explain the basics of weather.

Gutnik, Martin J. Experiments That Explore the Greenhouse Effect. 1991. illus. Millbrook, lib. ed., $14.40 (1-56294-013-9).

Gr. 5–8. Gutnik discusses the properties of air, the causes of the greenhouse effect, and the results of global warming and presents 10 experiments. *Experiments That Explore Oil Spills* is another volume in this clearly written series.

Hecht, Jeff. Shifting Shores: Rising Seas, Retreating Coastlines. 1990. illus. Scribner, $14.95 (0-684-19087-7).

Gr. 6–12. Covering topics from beach erosion to global warming, Hecht explains how oceans, lakes, and rivers change the land along their shores. This well-written book includes many maps, tables, and black-and-white photos.

Hiscock, Bruce. The Big Storm. 1993. illus. Atheneum, $14.95 (0-689-31770-0).

Gr. 2–5. Bright watercolor paintings illustrate this informative picture book, which chronicles the course of a devastating storm in 1982: heavy rains along the Pacific Coast, avalanches in the Sierra Nevada, blizzards in the Rockies, tornadoes in the Midwest, and deep snow from the Great Lakes to the East Coast.

Horenstein, Sidney. Rocks Tell Stories: Beyond Museum Walls. 1993. illus. Millbrook, $15.40 (1-56294-238-7); paper, $6.95 (1-56294-766-4).

Gr. 4–7. Illustrated with full-color photos and diagrams, this book concisely discusses rocks, erosion, land formations, shifting continents, fossils, and rock collecting.

Johnson, Rebecca L. Investigating the Ozone Hole. 1994. illus. Lerner, $23.95 (0-8225-1574-1).

Gr. 5–8. This book discusses the development, discovery, and implications of the ozone hole located above Antarctica and takes readers to the South Pole to watch the researchers at work. Clear, colorful photographs and diagrams make this an attractive introduction to the subject.

Kahl, Jonathan D. Wet Weather: Rain Showers and Snowfall. 1992. illus. Lerner, lib. ed., $19.95 (0-8225-2526-7).

Gr. 4–6. Writing conversationally but precisely, Kahl explains scientific concepts with concrete, familiar examples. Well designed and illustrated with many colorful photos, tables, and diagrams, the books in this series include *Weatherwise: Learning about the Weather* and *Thunderbolt: Learning about Lightning*.

Kramer, Stephen. Avalanche. 1992. illus. Carolrhoda, lib. ed., $17.50 (0-87614-422-9).

Gr. 3–6. Using a question-and-answer format, *Avalanche* examines types of snowslides, describes how and why they occur, and explains what can be done to control them. Many full-color photos illustrate this clearly written book. Other volumes in the series include Kramer's *Lightning* and *Tornado* and Souza's *Powerful Waves*.

Lampton, Christopher. Volcano. 1991. illus. Millbrook, lib. ed., $13.90 (1-56294-028-7); paper, $5.95 (1-56294-786-9).

Gr. 4–7. This book explains the formation of different types of volcanoes and the types of eruptions that can occur. With sharp color photos and diagrams, uncluttered pages, and dynamic subjects, the volumes in the disaster series include *Drought, Earthquake, Hurricane, Tidal Wave,* and *Tornado.*

Lasky, Kathryn. Illus. by **Knight, Christopher G.** Surtsey: The Newest Place on Earth. 1992. Hyperion; dist. by Little, Brown, $15.95 (1-56282-300-0); lib. ed., $15.89 (1-56282-301-9); paper, $6.95 (0-7868-1004-1).

Gr. 5–8. This beautifully designed and well-written book documents the dramatic beginnings of the island of Surtsey. The many crisp photographs record the island's furious volcanic birth in 1963 and the changes occurring as the storm of ash dissipates, the fires cool, and life gradually establishes itself on shore.

Lee, Sally. Hurricanes. 1993. illus. Watts, lib. ed., $12.90 (0-531-20152-X); paper, $5.95 (0-531-15665-6).

Gr. 3–6. Written in a clear, readable style, this book describes the formation, structure, tracking, devastation, and forecasting of hurricanes. First-rate, full-color diagrams as well as photos, enhanced satellite images, and maps illustrate the text. Armbruster and Taylor's *Tornadoes,* Newton's *Earthquakes,* and Vogt's *Volcanoes* are related books in the First Book series.

Markle, Sandra. Earth Alive! 1991. illus. Lothrop, $14.95 (0-688-09360-4); lib. ed., $14.88 (0-688-09361-2).

Gr. 3–6. Several informal photo-essays about volcanoes, glaciers, earthquakes, and other cataclysmic movements dramatize the excitement of geological change. The beautifully reproduced color photographs heighten awareness of shapes and relationships in rock and sky.

Markle, Sandra. A Rainy Day. 1993. illus. Orchard, $14.95 (0-531-05976-6); lib. ed., $14.99 (0-531-08576-7).

Gr. K–3. As a young girl in a yellow slicker explores her world before, during, and after rain falls, the text offers simple scientific explanations of how clouds form, why rain falls, where the colors in the rainbow come from, and more.

McMillan, Bruce. The Weather Sky. 1991. illus. Farrar, $16.95 (0-374-38261-1).

Gr. 4–6. While its shape, size, and jacket suggest a picture book, this attractive photo-essay is actually one of the more challenging children's books on clouds and weather: challenging in the best sense, because readers willing to follow McMillan's explanation will come away with a fuller understanding.

McVey, Vicki. Illus. by **Weston, Martha.** The Sierra Club Book of Weatherwisdom. 1991. Sierra Club; dist. by Little, Brown, $16.95 (0-316-56341-2).

Gr. 4–7. McVey intersperses information about the earth, its atmosphere, and its climate with stories about children in different parts of the world who use significant weather signs to help themselves and those they love. This appealing book is written in a bright, conversational style and illustrated with pencil drawings on nearly every page.

Peters, Lisa Westberg. Meg and Dad Discover Treasure in the Air. 1995. illus. Holt, $15.95 (0-8050-2418-2).

Ages 5–7. In this picture book, Meg and her dad take a walk in the woods, where they find "rocks that look like stacks of lumpy pancakes." Her dad explains the creation of these fossils and their role in creating the earth's oxygen.

Peters, Lisa Westberg. Illus. by **Rand, Ted.** Water's Way. 1991. Arcade; dist. by Little, Brown, $14.95 (1-55970-062-9).

Ages 5–8. This picture book draws relationships between natural phenomena in the child's domain and in the larger world. Large paintings show how water changes form outdoors, while an inset picture shows parallel events happening in Tony's house on the same rainy day. Tony notices condensation on the window and writes his name in it; drips streak downward as the rain begins to fall. The text leaves it to the child, parent, or teacher to draw inferences between parallel events.

Rauzon, Mark J. and **Bix, Cynthia Overbeck.** Water, Water Everywhere. 1994. illus. Sierra Club; dist. by Random, $14.95 (0-87156-598-6).

Gr. 1–3. Illustrated with many striking photos, this book conveys the importance of water in the life of the planet and the urgency of protecting this limited resource.

Richardson, Joy. The Water Cycle. 1992. illus. Watts, lib. ed., $11.40 (0-531-14205-1).

K–Gr.2. In large type and short paragraphs, this simple science book on the water cycle discusses water as liquid, vapor, and solid and explains the formation of rain, snow, and clouds, as well as water treatment and recycling. Also in this series is Richardson's The Weather.

Sattler, Helen Roney. Illus. by **Maestro, Giulio.** Our Patchwork Planet: The Story of Plate Tectonics. 1995. Lothrop, $16 (0-688-09312-4); lib. ed., $15.93 (0-688-09313-2).

Gr. 4–8. Instead of fixing on particular volcanoes, mountains, or earthquakes, Sattler conveys the movement of the whole, with tectonic plates that resemble "vanilla wafers on top of chocolate pudding." Satellite photos give a global perspective, but it's the writing that gives readers the sense of the ground moving beneath their feet.

Schmid, Eleonore. The Living Earth. 1994. illus. North-South, $14.95 (1-55858-298-3); lib. ed., $14.88 (1-55858-299-1).

K–Gr.3. As in The Water's Journey and The Air around Us, Schmid introduces a complex subject in a picture-book format. Beautifully detailed illustrations reveal the abundance of diverse plant and animal life that live in the soil and the cycle of renewal taking place just below the earth's surface.

Simon, Seymour. Deserts. 1990. illus. Morrow, $13.95 (0-688-07415-4); lib. ed., $13.88 (0-688-07416-2).

Gr. 2–5. Remarkable photos heighten the appeal of this study of deserts, which concerns itself mostly with North American examples—the Great Basin, the Mojave, the Sonoran, and the Chihuahuan. Simon defines the term *desert,* discusses why deserts occur, and describes how their climates and land formations differ. Other volumes in the series include *Mountains* and *Oceans.*

Simon, Seymour. Weather. 1993. illus. Morrow, $15 (0-688-10546-7); lib. ed., $14.93 (0-688-10547-5).

Gr. 4–6. In this well-designed book, beautiful color photographs and diagrams illustrate direct explanations of the atmosphere, cold and warm fronts, and the formation of snow and hail.

Stangl, Jean. Crystals and Crystal Gardens You Can Grow. 1990. illus. Watts, lib. ed., $12.90 (0-531-10889-9).

Gr. 4–6. Illustrated with exceptionally clear full-color photos and black-and-white drawings, this attractive book describes the nature and structure of crystals and offers activities for those who want to watch crystals form.

VanCleave, Janice. Janice VanCleave's Volcanoes: Mind-boggling Experiments You Can Turn into Science Fair Projects. 1994. illus. Wiley, paper, $9.95 (0-471-30811-0).

Gr. 3–6. VanCleave demonstrates the science of volcanoes in a series of fairly simple activities with names such as "Magma Flow," "Spud Launcher," and, yes, "Erupting Volcano." Another geology-related book in this useful series is *Janice VanCleave's Earthquakes.*

Van Rose, Susanna. The Earth Atlas. 1994. illus. Dorling Kindersley, $19.95 (1-56458-626-X).

Gr. 4–7. This very oversize volume looks at the earth's crust, the ocean floor, and kinds of rocks as well as the history of the earth. Colorful illustrations, such as cutaways of earth features and examples of natural structures, are mostly big and bold, surrounded by text and smaller pictures.

Walker, Sally M. Water Up, Water Down: The Hydrologic Cycle. 1992. illus. Carolrhoda, lib. ed., $19.95 (0-87614-695-7).

Gr. 3–6. A good overview of the state and movement of water on earth and in the atmosphere, this attractive volume describes the water cycle and illustrates it with clear, colorful pictures on nearly every page. Also from this series are Walker's *Glaciers: Ice on the Move* and *Volcanoes: Earth's Inner Fire.*

Waters, John F. Deep-Sea Vents. 1994. illus. Dutton/Cobblehill, $14.99 (0-525-65145-4).

Gr. 4–6. Illustrated with full-color photographs, this book discusses the terrain, water temperatures, and conditions favorable to life near deep-sea vents, as well as the bacteria and animals living there.

Whitfield, Philip. Why Do Volcanoes Erupt? 1990. illus. Viking, $16.95 (0-670-83385-1).

Gr. 5–7. Not only volcanoes, but all the mysterious forces shaping planet Earth are covered in this exhaustive text. Whitfield poses 139 questions, ranging from the basic ("What is the difference between geology and geography?") to the cosmic ("How did the Universe begin?"), and answers them in short paragraphs.

Wiggers, Raymond. The Amateur Geologist: Explorations and Investigations. 1993. illus. Watts, lib. ed., $12.90 (0-531-11112-1); paper, $6.95 (0-531-15695-8).

Gr. 6–10. Introducing the fundamentals of geology, this book presents basic facts and suggests activities for kids who want to explore the subject firsthand. From tracing the local drainage network to collecting and identifying rocks, and fossils, Wiggers proves an enthusiastic guide. Also in the series is Mogil and Levine's *Amateur Meteorologist.*

Prehistoric Life

Arnold, Caroline. Illus. by **Hewett, Richard.** Dinosaurs All Around: An Artist's View of the Prehistoric World. 1993. Clarion, lib. ed., $14.95 (0-395-62363-4).

Gr. 3–6. Featuring paleoartist Stephen Czerkas, whose miniatures and life-size replicas can be found in many museums, Arnold's intriguing book explores the craft of making dinosaur models. Photographs capture the intricacies of the modeling process and finished replicas of several different dinosaurs.

Arnold, Caroline. Illus. by **Hewett, Richard.** Dinosaurs Down Under and Other Fossils from Australia. 1990. Clarion, $15.45 (0-89919-814-7); paper, $6.95 (0-395-69119-2).

Gr. 3–6. This appealing dinosaur book highlights a museum display of the Kadimakara fossils of Australia. From the Aboriginal legend of the dreamtime creatures to prehistoric Australian vertebrates to the work of shipping, assembling, and displaying the fossils, this well-written book explores the subject, while the full-color photos capture the action and the mystery of it all.

Benton, Michael. Dinosaur and Other Prehistoric Animal Factfinder. 1992. illus. Kingfisher, paper, $12.95 (1-85697-802-8).

Gr. 3–6. Nicely designed, this fine quick-reference source profiles some 200 dinosaurs and other animals, including cats, birds, and rodents. Each entry includes a small but excellent painting or black-and-white sketch and a paragraph or two of text that pinpoints distinguishing features.

Bernstein, Joanne E. and **Cohen, Paul.** Why Didn't the Dinosaur Cross the Road and Other Prehistoric Riddles. 1990. illus. Albert Whitman, $8.95 (0-8075-9077-0).

Gr. 3–5. For a lighter (not to say giddy) approach to dinosaurs, this riddle book combines lively wordplay and cartoonlike illustrations to evoke groans of delight. "Question: Why did cave folks have wrinkled clothing? Answer: It wasn't the Iron Age yet."

Brenner, Barbara. Dinosaurium: The Museum That Explores the World of Living Dinosaurs. 1993. illus. Bantam, paper, $9.50 (0-553-35427-2).

Ages 6–10. Welcome to the imaginary Dinosaurium, where one can walk from one era to another and see lifelike models of dinosaurs and their habitats. Full-color drawings illustrate children and adults exploring the many wonders of life on earth 200 million years ago.

Cohen, Daniel and **Cohen, Susan.** Where to Find Dinosaurs Today. 1992. illus. Dutton/Cobblehill, $15 (0-525-65098-9); Puffin, paper, $6.99 (0-14-036154-5).

Gr. 5–7. An indispensable guide for any serious dinophile and a kick for the mildly curious, this guidebook (arranged by region) will point out places to visit, from Dinosaur National Monument and the National History Museum of the Smithsonian Institution to a store that sells replicas of dinosaur skulls.

Cole, Joanna. Illus. by **Degen, Bruce.** The Magic School Bus in the Time of the Dinosaurs. 1994. Scholastic, $14.95 (0-590-44688-6).

K–Gr.4. Ms. Frizzle loads up the

school bus for a hair-raising journey through the Triassic, Jurassic, and Cretaceous periods. The pages brim with dinosaur facts and theories, wisecracking dialogue, and energetic illustrations.

Dewan, Ted. Inside Dinosaurs and Other Prehistoric Creatures. 1994. illus. Doubleday, $16.95 (0-385-31143-5).

Gr. 4–7. Stripping away the skin to look inside dinosaurs, this colorfully illustrated book looks at dino dentition, respiration, locomotion, skeletons and much more.

Dodson, Peter. An Alphabet of Dinosaurs. 1995. illus. Scholastic, $14.95 (0-590-46486-8).

Gr. 2–4. A brief text introduces 26 dinosaurs, while dramatic paintings use vivid colors and minute details to create fantastic scenes of dinosaur days. Precise black-and-white drawings show skeletons and details of bones.

Funston, Sylvia. The Dinosaur Question and Answer Book. 1992. illus. Little, Brown/Joy Street, $16.95 (0-316-67736-1).

Gr. 4–6. The editors of *Owl* and *Chickadee* magazines collaborated with the Dinosaur Project (a joint venture of Chinese and Canadian scientists) to answer the children's questions about dinosaurs. Photos, drawings, and cartoons brighten this inviting book.

Gillette, J. Lynett. The Search for Seismosaurus: The World's Longest Dinosaur. 1994. illus. Dial, $14.99 (0-8037-1358-4); lib. ed., $14.89 (0-8037-1359-2).

Gr. 3–6. This fascinating, though sometimes rather technical account of unearthing seismosaurus takes readers to the site as scientists conduct the painstaking work that often yields more frustrations than finds. Good color photographs document the gritty, monoto-

nous work of the dino diggers, while Mark Hallett's beautiful paintings are sure to spark imaginations.

Horner, John R. and **Lessem, Don**. Digging up Tyrannosaurus Rex. 1992. illus. Crown, $14.99 (0-517-58783-1); lib. ed., $14.99 (0-517-58784-X).

Gr. 4–7. Paleontologist Horner and science journalist Lessem describe the discovery and excavation of the first complete *Tyrannosaurus rex* skeleton ever found. With many color photographs, this appealing book invites browsers and rewards readers.

Lasky, Kathryn. Dinosaur Dig. 1990. illus. Morrow, $13.95 (0-688-08574-1); lib. ed., $13.88 (0-688-08575-X).

Gr. 4–7. This photo-essay transports readers to the Montana Badlands, where the author's family joins a dinosaur dig. Vivid full-color photographs capture the work, the dangers, and the excitement of the experience.

Lasky, Kathryn. Traces of Life: The Origins of Humankind. 1990. illus. Morrow, $16.95 (0-688-07237-2).

Gr. 5–8. Creating an imaginary clock in which one hour equals 200 million years, Lasky traces the timeline of life's development on the earth. Photographs and precise drawings of excavations sites, fossils, and the ever-evolving human illustrate this authoritative yet highly readable book.

Lauber, Patricia. Living with Dinosaurs. 1991. illus. Bradbury, $16.95 (0-02-754521-0).

Gr. 3–7. This well-researched book re-creates what Montana was like 75 million years ago: a warm, shallow sea cuts North America in two, the Rocky Mountains are being born, dinosaurs rule the land, and other creatures share it with them. Best of all, the last chapter (on fossils) explains how we know what it was like so long ago.

Lessem, Don and **Glut, Donald F.** The Dinosaur Society's Dinosaur Encyclopedia. 1993. illus. Random, $25 (0-679-41770-2).

Gr. 5–9. A fine, illustrated guide to the more than 600 known dinosaurs, this volume dispels myths, discusses current knowledge and ongoing questions, and introduces the dinosaurs themselves.

Lessem, Don. Jack Horner: Living with Dinosaurs. 1994. illus. W. H. Freeman, $14.95 (0-7167-6546-2).

Gr. 4–7. This highly readable biography tells of Jack Horner, who loved dinosaurs from the beginning and knew that studying them would be his lifework. An undiagnosed dyslexic, Horner flunked out of college several times, but he persevered to become one of the world's leading dinosaur experts.

Lindsay, William. Triceratops. 1993. illus. Dorling Kindersley, $12.95 (1-56458-226-4).

Gr. 3–6. Specially created scale models, detailed drawings, and vintage photographs bring to life the discovery and excavation of fossils and the daily life of Triceratops. Other volumes in the series include *Barosaurus* and *Tyrannosaurus*.

McGowan, Chris. Discover Dinosaurs. 1993. illus. Addison-Wesley, paper, $9.95 (0-201-62267-X).

Gr. 4–6. Would-be dinosaur detectives and plain old dinosaur lovers will find plenty to investigate and ponder here, in nine compact chapters with colorful illustrations. The concepts are well defined for the intended audience, though many of the activities and experiments will require adult supervision.

Most, Bernard. Where to Look for a Dinosaur. 1993. illus. Harcourt, $12.95 (0-15-295616-6).

Gr. 1–4. This geographical guide-book pinpoints the remains of more than 25 beasts and looks at what each of these dinosaurs would find its habitat to be like were it alive now. The arctosaurus, for example, would find itself near the chilly Arctic Circle, while the alamosaurus would awake in Texas near the famous San Antonio fort.

Mullins, Patricia. Dinosaur Encore. 1993. illus. HarperCollins/Willa Perlman, $15 (0-06-021069-9).

K–Gr.3. Comparing living animals with dinosaurs, this clever book includes foldout pages and tissue-paper collages with an exciting, three-dimensional feeling.

Penner, Lucille Recht. Dinosaur Babies. 1991. illus. Random, lib. ed., $7.99 (0-679-91207-X); paper, $3.50 (0-679-81207-5).

K–Gr.2. From the Step into Reading series, this presents sound information about dinosaurs and their babies. Beginning readers will like the large type and the many pictures of dinosaurs in action.

Sattler, Helen Roney. The New Illustrated Dinosaur Dictionary. 1990. illus. Lothrop, $24.95 (0-688-08462-1).

Gr. 5–9. Anyone who confuses *pteranodon* and *pterodactyl* can sort them out with this impressive handbook, which describes 350 dinosaurs and provides general information under headings such as Food, Size, and Teeth.

Sattler, Helen Roney. Stegosaurs: The Solar-Powered Dinosaurs. 1992. illus. Lothrop, $15 (0-688-10055-4); lib. ed., $14.93 (0-688-10056-2).

Gr. 2–5. In a highly readable book illustrated with full-color paintings, Sattler introduces the apparently slow-witted and ungainly stegosaurus, a highly successful dinosaur.

Schlein, Miriam. Discovering Dinosaur Babies. 1991. illus. Four Winds, $14.95 (0-02-778091-0).

Gr. 2–4. Making clear the difficulties of interpreting fossil finds, this intriguing book explains what is known about dinosaur offspring and how their parents cared for them. Boldly executed paintings are scattered throughout the book.

Schlein, Miriam. Let's Go Dinosaur Tracking! 1991. illus. HarperCollins, lib. ed., $14.89 (0-06-025139-5).

Gr. 2–4. Bright, playful illustrations show a grandfather and three spirited children who don boots, helmets, and canteens before setting off in search of dinosaur tracks. In simple language, readers learn how tracks are made and preserved as well as what scientists learn from them.

VanCleave, Janice. Dinosaurs for Every Kid: Easy Activities That Make Learning Science Fun. 1994. illus. Wiley, $24.95 (0-471-30813-7); paper, $10.95 (0-471-30812-9).

Gr. 4–7. In 20 informative chapters with many activities for learning, VanCleave explores the known and unknown about dinosaurs, including how fossils are formed, the meanings of dinosaur names, theories about dinosaur skin, and how a dinosaur's weight is determined.

The Visual Dictionary of Dinosaurs. 1993. illus. Dorling Kindersley, $15.95 (1-56458-188-8).

Gr. 4–6. Illustrated with many brightly colored pictures and charts, this book explains the vocabulary of dinosaur anatomy and classification. Two-page spreads explore geological periods from the Triassic to the Cretaceous.

Weishampel, David B. Plant-eating Dinosaurs. 1992. illus. Watts, lib. ed., $14.90 (0-531-11021-4).

Gr. 4–6. Ferocious meat-eaters usually grab all the glory in children's books about dinosaurs. Here Weishampel shares his enthusiasm for plant-eating dinosaurs, discussing what they ate and how they survived for more than 160 million years.

Whitfield, Philip. Macmillan Children's Guide to Dinosaurs and Other Prehistoric Animals. 1992. illus. Macmillan, $16.95 (0-02-762362-9).

Gr. 3–6. Handsomely illustrated and well designed, the guide is a catalog of prehistoric animal life and a source of basic information on 125 dinosaurs and their kin.

Whitfield, Philip. Why Did the Dinosaurs Disappear? 1991. illus. Viking, $16.95 (0-670-84055-6).

Gr. 5–7. Why *did* the dinosaurs disappear? Whitfield presents the usual theories, then follows up with other topics in a question-and-answer format. Why are there different races of humans? Was there a real place called Atlantis? How did the giraffe get its long neck? Clear writing, drawings, and photographs make this an inviting book.

Wilkes, Angela. The Big Book of Dinosaurs: A First Book for Young Children. 1994. illus. Dorling Kindersley, $12.95 (1-56458-718-5).

K–Gr.2. This could be called *The Really Big Book of Dinosaurs* since its size is as awesome as the animals it showcases. The big, handsome photographs and drawings accompany the simple introductory text of this visually appealing book.

Life Science

Arnold, Caroline. Watching Desert Wildlife. 1994. illus. Carolrhoda, lib. ed., $14.96 (0-87614-841-0).

Gr. 3–6. Clear photos illustrate this introduction to what deserts are and how they work as ecosystems as well as the wildlife they sustain.

Arnosky, Jim. Crinkleroot's Guide to Walking in Wild Places. 1990. illus. Bradbury, $14.95 (0-02-705842-5).

Gr. 1–4. Amiable woodsman Crinkleroot tells youngsters how to walk safely through the wild without bothering its inhabitants or being fearful of little things like snakes, ticks, and poison ivy. Brisk ink-and-wash drawings accurately depict the plants and critters of the woodland.

Aronson, Billy. They Came from DNA. 1993. illus. W. H. Freeman, $19.95 (0-7167-9006-8); paper, $13.95 (0-7167-6526-8).

Gr. 3–6. Charged by Intergalactic Intelligence with finding out "what makes Earth creatures what they are," alien Skreeg investigates and slowly begins to understand evolution and the key to the mysteries he is investigating: the structure and function of DNA. And, with a little luck and perseverance, readers will, too. Colorful illustrations underscore the author's offbeat humor and help readers visualize the science.

Banks, Martin. Conserving Rain Forests. 1990. illus. Steck-Vaughn, lib. ed., $21.34 (0-8114-2387-5); paper, $5.95 (0-8114-3452-4).

Gr. 3–6. This well-organized book introduces rain forests: their makeup, their wildlife, their locations, their importance, and the forces that threaten them. Many photos and maps illustrate the book.

Bendick, Jeanne. Exploring an Ocean Tide Pool. 1992. illus. Holt/Redfeather, $14.95 (0-8050-2043-8).

Gr. 3–5. Bendick introduces the plants and animals of the tide pool, discussing their food web as well as their adaptations to this unique ecosystem. Full-color photographs and excellent black-and-white drawings and diagrams illustrate this attractive handbook.

Bryan, Jenny. Genetic Engineering. 1995. illus. Thomson Learning, lib. ed., $15.95 (1-56847-268-4).

Gr. 7–9. Illustrated with photographs, this timely book presents the complex topic of genetic engineering with impressive lucidity and evenhandedness.

Burns, Diane L. Rocky Mountain Seasons: From Valley to Mountaintop. 1993. Macmillan, $14.95 (0-02-716142-0).

Gr. 2–6. Burns describes seasonal changes in the Rocky Mountains. The book begins in the spring. The photography is excellent and will certainly draw readers into Burns' evocative chronicle.

Cherry, Lynne. The Great Kapok Tree: A Tale of the Amazon Rain Forest. 1990. illus. Harcourt/Gulliver, $14.95 (0-15-200520-X).

K–Gr.3. A man enters the Brazilian rain forest to chop down a tree. When he falls asleep, the animals crowd around, expressing the tragic impact the loss will have on the ecosystem. With its large format and striking, full-color artwork this picture book is a real eye-opener.

Cole, Joanna. Illus. by **Degen, Bruce**. The Magic School Bus on the Ocean Floor. 1992. Scholastic, $19.95 (0-590-41430-5); paper, $4.95 (0-590-41431-3).

Gr. 1–5. Wild and wacky teacher Ms. Frizzle takes her class on a fact-finding mission to the ocean floor. This science book has it all: colorful artwork, zany story, straightforward text, comical comments from the cartoonlike characters, hidden semaphore messages, and even facts about the ocean and its undersea life.

Crenson, Victoria. Bay Shore Park: The Death and Life of an Amusement Park. 1995. illus. W. H. Freeman, $16.95 (0-7167-6580-2).

Gr. 4–6. Illustrated with detailed watercolors and black-and-white drawings, this intriguing natural history book demonstrates natural succession as it visits the site of an amusement park which closed nearly 50 years ago and demonstrates how plants and animals have reclaimed the land.

Dewey, Jennifer Owings. A Night and Day in the Desert. 1991. illus. Little, Brown, $15.95 (0-316-18210-9).

Gr. 2–5. Stressing food chains, life cycles, interdependence, and adaptation to the environment, the lively text shows the natural order of things in the desert, both during the day and at night. Dewey's colored-pencil drawings effectively illustrate the book.

Dorros, Arthur. Rain Forest Secrets. 1990. illus. Scholastic, $14.95 (0-590-43369-5).

Gr. 3–5. Written in a conversational tone, this picture book introduces rain forests (temperate as well as tropical), describing their special features and importance to the environment. Effective pen-and-wash drawings suggest the lush greenery of the rain forests.

Downer, Ann. Spring Pool: A Guide to the Ecology of Temporary Ponds. 1992. illus. Watts, $15.95 (0-531-15251-0); lib. ed., $15.90 (0-531-11150-4).

Gr. 5–8. This attractive book intro-duces readers to temporary ponds, little-known but important and endangered habitats for many forms of aquatic life, including salamanders, a variety of insects, and wood frogs.

Dvorak, David. A Sea of Grass: The Tallgrass Prairie. 1994. illus. Macmillan, $14.95 (0-02-733245-4).

Gr. 2–4. In pictures of glowing color and a spare, sometimes poetic text, this photo-essay celebrates the tallgrass prairie and warns that it is in danger of extinction. As the seasons change, Dvorak captures the open landscape and the immense variety of plants and animals, indicating the essential connections between them, the delicate balance that is threatened.

Evans, J. Edward. Charles Darwin: Revolutionary Biologist. 1993. illus. Lerner, $21.50 (0-8225-4914-X).

Gr. 6–9. As Evans states, "The brush-fire of controversy set off by the publication of *The Origin of Species* has never been extinguished." Illustrated wtih black-and-white photos and prints, this biography tells of Darwin's youth, travels, research, conclusions, publications, and legacy.

Few, Roger. The Atlas of Wild Places: In Search of the Earth's Last Wildernesses. 1994. illus. Facts On File, $35 (0-8160-3168-1).

Gr. 5–8. With gorgeous pictures and practically no maps, this may not be an atlas, but it is a handsome book introducing 53 wilderness areas around the world.

Flatt, Lizann. My First Nature Treasury. 1995. illus. Sierra Club; dist. by Random, $12.95 (0-87156-362-2).

K–Gr.3. From the editors of *Chickadee* magazine, this large-format book introduces biomes, ecosystems, the food chain, and the classifications of plants and animals. Readers are invited

27

to find inhabitants of biomes in the big, colorful illustrations.

Forsyth, Adrian. How Monkeys Make Chocolate: Foods and Medicines from the Rainforests. 1995. illus. Firefly, $16.95 (1-895688-45-0); paper, $9.95 (1-895688-32-9).

Gr. 5–8. A Canadian biologist combines a sense of wonder with a wealth of factual information as he writes about rain forests around the world, each a unique web of plants and animals and people that depend on each other for survival. The large volume is designed like a glossy magazine, with fully captioned color photos and framed insets in the detailed text.

George, Jean Craighead. Illus. by **Minor, Wendell.** Everglades. 1995. HarperCollins, $14.95 (0-06-021228-4); lib. ed., $14.89 (0-06-021229-2).

Gr. 2–4. Illustrated with full-page paintings, this handsome book celebrates the beauty of the Everglades before humans damaged the ecosystem, shows what it may have looked like teeming with plants and animals, and encourages children to restore the environment.

George, Jean Craighead. One Day in the Tropical Rain Forest. 1990. illus. HarperCollins/Crowell, $14 (0-690-04767-3); lib. ed., $13.89 (0-690-04769-X).

Gr. 3–6. From the author's One Day series, this book is a vivid portrait of a rain forest through an illustrated narrative written as a log book, noting the interactions between prople, animals, and machines over the couse of a day.

Gibbons, Gail. Nature's Green Umbrella: Tropical Rain Forests. 1994. illus. Morrow, $15 (0-688-12353-8); lib. ed., $14.93 (0-688-12354-6).

Gr. 3–5. Simply written and colorfully illustrated, this book not only explains the complex ecosystem of tropical rain forests and their importance to the global ecology, but also explores related issues concerning preservation and protection of the forests.

Goodman, Susan E. Bats, Bugs, and Biodiversity: Adventures in the Amazonian Rain Forest. 1995. Simon & Schuster/Atheneum, $16 (0-689-31942-6).

This photo-essay records the experiences of seventh - and eighth-grade students from Michigan who traveled to the Peruvian Amazon. Clear, full-color photos focus on the children's experiences as well as on the environment and people they came to know.

Guerrini, Francesco. The Great Book of the Sea: A Complete Guide to Marine Life. 1993. illus. Running Press/Courage, $29.98 (1-56138-270-1).

Gr. 6–12. First published in Italy, this comprehensive guide to marine life offers sections on invertebrates, fish, reptiles, birds, and mammals. Geographic-distribution maps accompany most of the entries. With an informative text and more than 1,000 full-color illustrations, this will prove a valuable and easy-to-use reference resource for older students.

Guiberson, Brenda Z. Cactus Hotel. 1991. Holt, $15.95 (0-8050-1333-4); paper, $4.95 (0-8050-2960-5).

K–Gr.3. Written with simplicity, this book follows 150 years in the life of a giant saguaro cactus, which grows from a tiny seed to a giant cactus that serves as a home for a variety of birds, bats, insects, and rats. Crisp, attractive illustrations in colored pencil and watercolor show the beauty of the desert landscape and its variety of wildlife.

Hirschi, Ron. Save Our Wetlands. 1994. illus. Doubleday, $17.95 (0-385-31152-4); paper, $9.95 (0-385-31197-4).

Gr. 4–8. Illustrated with fine color

photographs, this book describes various kinds of wetlands, their animals and plants, and the problems faced by wetland habitats. Other books in the Audubon One Earth Book series include Hirschi's *Save Our Oceans and Coasts* and *Save Our Prairies and Grasslands*.

Jenike, David and **Jenike, Mark**. A Walk through a Rain Forest: Life in the Ituri Forest of Zaire. 1995. illus. Watts, lib. ed., $14.91 (0-531-11168-7); paper, $9.95 (0-531-15721-0).

Gr.4–7. Readers gain a real sense of the indigenous people and the extraordinary plant and animal life of the Ituri Forest as they journey with a young boy and his grandparents from their small village to an outlying fishing camp. The colorful, captioned photos include many close-ups of forest animals.

Johnson, Rebecca L. The Great Barrier Reef: A Living Laboratory. 1992. illus. Lerner, $21.50 (0-8225-1596-2).

Gr. 5–8. In short, well-written chapters, Johnson captures the excitement of the scientists conducting research along Australia's Great Barrier Reef, the world's largest coral reef.

Kuhn, Dwight. My First Book of Nature: How Living Things Grow. 1993. illus. Scholastic, $11.95 (0-590-45502-8).

K–Gr.3. More for browsing than for research, this introduction to the natural world provides close-ups of five plants, including mushrooms and apple trees, and 25 animals, from earthworms to humans. Exceptionally fine photos illustrate the brief text.

Lampton, Christopher. Coral Reefs in Danger. 1992. illus. Millbrook, lib. ed., $15.40 (1-56294-091-0).

Gr. 4–6. Lampton explains how coral reefs are formed, describes the symbiotic relationships in their ecosystem, and presents a convincing argument that global warming may be responsible for the bleaching that is killing them. Excellent color photos illustrate the book.

Landau, Elaine. Tropical Rain Forests around the World. 1990. illus. Watts, lib. ed., $12.90 (0-531-10896-1); paper, $5.95 (0-531-15600-1).

Gr. 3–6. This book offers a good, simple discussion of tropical rain forests and the plants and animals that make up these ecosystems.

Lauber, Patricia. Summer of Fire: Yellowstone, 1988. 1991. illus. Watts/Orchard, $17.95 (0-531-05943-X); lib. ed., $17.99 (0-531-08543-0).

Gr. 3–6. Beginning with the striking photograph on the jacket, this book provides vivid glimpses and cogent discussion of the Yellowstone National Park fires of 1988 and their aftermath.

Lauber, Patricia. Who Eats What? Food Chains and Food Webs. 1995. illus. HarperCollins, $15 (0-06-022981-0); lib. ed., $4.95 (0-06-445130-5).

K–Gr.3. Ink-and-watercolor drawings illustrate this simple presentation of food chains and food webs on land and under water. Besides showing who eats what in the wild, it brings the ideas closer to home with the suggestion that children draw pictures showing the chains for the things they eat, such as their milk, which came from a cow, which ate grass.

Lessem, Don. Inside the Amazing Amazon. 1995. illus. Crown, $18 (0-517-59490-0).

Gr. 4–6. This large-format book focuses on the distinct layers of the Amazon rain forest and the plants and animals living in each one.

Liptak, Karen. Saving Our Wetlands and Their Wildlife. 1991. illus. Watts, lib. ed., $12.90 (0-531-20092-2); paper, $5.95 (0-531-15648-6).

Gr. 4–7. Explaining the differences

between fresh- and salt-water wetlands, this book describes the unique ecosystems of estuaries, swamps, marshes, bogs, and bottomlands. Colorful photographs reflect the variety of plants and animals described.

Lourie, Peter. Everglades: Buffalo Tiger and the River of Grass. 1994. illus. Boyds Mills, $16.95 (1-878093-91-6).

Gr. 4–7. Lourie offers an illustrated tour of the Everglades, the "River of Grass," guided by a Miccosukee Indian, who provides insight into what the area has meant to his people.

Luenn, Nancy. Illus. by **Himler, Ronald**. Squish! A Wetland Walk. 1994. Atheneum, $14.95 (0-689-31842-1).

K–Gr.2. A feast for the senses, this book introduces the sights, sounds, and smells of a wetland as experienced by a young boy. Luenn uses simple language to explain some of the many ways wetlands are beneficial, while Himler's quiet watercolors capture the atmosphere.

Mallory, Kenneth. Water Hole: Life in a Rescued Tropical Forest. 1992. illus. Watts, $15.95 (0-531-15250-2); lib. ed., $15.90 (0-531-11154-7).

Gr. 5–8. Following a coatis (a raccoonlike animal) from water hole to water hole, Mallory highlights the reclamation of a tropical forest in Costa Rica and introduces a variety of indigenous plants and animals. The captioned, color photographs are beautifully reproduced.

McMillan, Bruce. Summer Ice: Life along the Antarctic Peninsula. 1995. illus. Houghton, $15.95 (0-395-66561-2).

Gr. 4–6. Illustrated with exceptionally clear, full-color photos, this book introduces the Antarctic Peninsula: the landforms, the glacial iceforms, and the unexpected wealth of summer wildlife.

Mills, Patricia. On an Island in the Bay. 1994. illus. North-South, $14.95 (1-55858-333-5); lib. ed., $14.88 (1-55858-334-3).

K–Gr.3. With color photos and precise, lyrical captions, this quiet, beautiful photo-essay celebrates the remote islands of Chesapeake Bay. Mills captures the sweep and the fragility of the island environment, from the early morning view of sky and shore to the close-up of a lone heron in the noonday sun.

Myers, Christopher A and **Myers, Lynne Born**. McCrephy's Field. 1991. illus. Houghton, $14.45 (0-395-53807-6).

Gr. 1–3. When Joe McCrephy leaves his Ohio farm, the empty cornfield is gradually covered with grass and flowers, which give way to small trees and bushes, and, ultimately, to woods. This lesson in natural succession unfolds easily through a personable narrative and skillful watercolors that reflect a keen sense of the land.

Norsgaard, E. Jaediker. Nature's Great Balancing Act: In Our Own Backyard. 1990. illus. Dutton/Cobblehill, $14.95 (0-525-65028-8).

Gr. 4–6. The authors discuss the balance of nature (including food chains) in terms of their backyard, a habitat supporting birds, insects, and animals. Revealing color photos support the clearly written text.

Patent, Dorothy Hinshaw. Illus. by **Muñoz, William**. Yellowstone Fires: Flames and Rebirth. 1990. Holiday, $14.95 (0-8234-0807-8).

Gr. 2–6. Illustrated with photographs and written in clear, thoughtful language, this book discusses the controversy relating to forest fires and explains that fires are only one stage in the continuing evolution of any forest.

Pringle, Lawrence. Coral Reefs: Earth's Undersea Treasures. 1995. illus. Simon

& Schuster, $16 (0-689-80286-2).

Gr. 4–6. Illustrated with clear, colorful photos, this well-written book explores the variety of life in coral reefs.

Pringle, Laurence. Illus. by **Marstall, Bob**. Fire in the Forest: A Cycle of Growth and Renewal. 1995. Simon & Schuster/Atheneum, $16 (0-689-80394-X).

Gr. 4–6. Chiding news commentators for calling the 1988 forest fires in Yellowstone National Park catastrophic, Pringle discusses the effect of fires on the plants and animals native to the region and shows that fire is simply part of the ecosystem's natural cycle. Vivid paintings show the same landscape in different stages of growth before, during, and after a fire.

Quinlan, Susan. The Case of the Mummified Pigs and Other Mysteries in Nature. 1995. illus. Boyds Mills; dist. by St. Martin's, $15.95 (1-878093-82-7).

Gr. 4–6. Why are monarch butterflies so brightly colored? What happened to the burgeoning reindeer herd on isolated Saint Matthew Island? In a quiet yet dramatic fashion, Quinlan follows the scientists who sought solutions to these and 12 other puzzling occurrences, vividly demonstrating the intricate linkage between plants and animals that exists in nature.

Reef, Catherine. Rachel Carson: A Wonder of Nature. 1991. illus. Twenty-First Century, lib. ed., $14.95 (0-941477-38-X).

Gr. 2–5. Using a fairly simple vocabulary, Reef describes the life and significant contributions of the biologist whose books awakened her generation to environmental awareness. Attractive pencil drawings illustrate the story. Other biographies in the series include Reef's *Henry David Thoreau: A Neighbor to Nature* and *Jacques Cousteau: Champion of the Sea*, as well as Teresa

Rogers' *George Washington Carver: Nature's Trailblazer*.

Rood, Ronald. Wetlands. 1994. illus. HarperCollins, $15 (0-06-023010-X); lib. ed., $14.89 (0-06-023011-8).

Gr. 3–5. This inviting little book introduces the plants and animals of freshwater wetlands. With relatively large print and wide spaces between lines, the pages have an inviting look, enhanced by the softly shaded watercolor illustrations appearing on nearly every page. Readers will find this an engaging introduction to the ecology of "swamps and streams and soggy places." Other books in the Nature Studies series include Rood's *Tide Pools* and Jonathan Pine's *Backyard Birds*.

Sayre, April Pulley. Tropical Rain Forest. 1994. illus. Twenty-First Century, $15.95 (0-8050-2826-9).

Gr. 4–7. Illustrated with full-color photos, this lively, informative book explores the complex ecosystem of the tropical rain forest. Others in the Exploring Earth's Biomes series include Sayre's *Desert, Grassland, Taiga, Temperate Deciduous Forest,* and *Tundra*.

Shades of Green. Ed. by Anne Harvey. 1992. illus. Greenwillow, $18 (0-688-10890-3.

Gr. 4–8. This handsome volume includes 200 poems, both classic and contemporary, that celebrate nature in all its power and fragility.

Shulman, Jeffrey. Gaylord Nelson: A Day for the Earth. 1991. illus. Twenty-First Century, lib. ed., $14.95 (0-941477-40-1).

Gr. 2–5. Honoring the founder of Earth Day, this biography traces the environmentalist's life from boyhood antics in his small Wisconsin town to his influence as the state's governor and as a U.S. senator, notably his proposal for "a national teach-in on the crisis of the environment."

Siebert, Diane. Illus. by **Minor, Wendell.** Sierra. 1991. HarperCollins, $16 (0-06-021639-5); lib. ed., $15.89 (0-06-021640-9).

Ages 5–8. This picture book expresses the majesty of the Sierra Nevada with solemn, lyrical couplets and breathtaking illustrations. The book encompasses spacious landscapes, yet includes detailed portraits of creatures great and small in both the verse and the paintings.

Silver, Donald M. Pond: One Small Square. 1995. illus. W. H. Freeman, $14.95 (0-7167-6518-7).

Gr. 2–5. This colorfully illustrated book encourages children to observe the plants and animals that live in, on, above, and around a pond. With safety concerns and respect for wildlife apparent, it shows children how to measure off a 24-inch square for observation, keep a notebook, look underwater with a homemade viewer, examine mud dwellers, and make a diorama. Other books in the One Small Square series include *Arctic Tundra, African Savanna, Backyard, Cave,* and *Seashore.*

Staub, Frank. America's Wetlands. 1995. illus. Carolrhoda, lib. ed., $14.96 (0-87614-827-5).

Gr. 4–6. This informative book describes types of North American wetlands and discusses their importance in the ecosystem. On every page, colorful photographs illustrate the many kinds of wetlands in the U.S. and the plants and animals that thrive in these habitats. Another book in the Earth Watch series is Staub's *America's Prairies.*

Swanson, Diane. Safari beneath the Sea: The Wonder World of the North Pacific Coast. 1994. illus. Sierra Club; dist. by Little, Brown, $16.95 (0-87156-415-7).

Gr. 4–8. Large, outstanding color photos make this a most appealing study of the inhabitants of the North Pacific coastal waters. The text describes wind currents, temperatures, and terrain and then discusses the strange habits of such familiar creatures as the octopus, sea anemone, jellyfish, slug, and sea urchin.

Taylor, Barbara. Pond Life. 1992. illus. Dorling Kindersley, $9.95 (1-879431-94-7).

Gr. 2–6. Illustrated with clear, colorful photographs that portray each species, often larger than life, this book spotlights notable animals and plants of the pond, including the water lily, dragonfly, newt, water boatman, stickleback, frog, and great pond snail. Most of the facts appear in captions. Other books in the Look Closer series include *Coral Reef, Desert Life, Meadow, Tide Pool,* and *Shoreline.*

Tesar, Jenny. Patterns in Nature: An Overview of the Living World. 1994. illus. Blackbirch, $15.95 (1-56711-058-4); paper, $6.95 (0-316-90249-7).

Gr. 5–7. The introductory book in the Our Living World series, this takes an ecosystem-wide view of nature, detailing interdependencies and the principles of classification. Clearly written, the book has excellent color photographs. Other books in the series include *Patterns, Microorganisms, Fungi, Crustaceans,* and *Resource Guide.*

Twist, Clint. Seas and Oceans. 1991. illus. Dillon, $15.95 (0-87518-491-X); paper, $6.95 (0-316-90249-7).

Gr. 5–8. With striking color photographs that are well suited to the oversize format, this book introduces the seas and oceans as habitats with interdependent plants and animals, shows how these environments are threatened, and raises possible solutions to specific problems. The Ecology Watch series also includes *Deserts* and *Rainforests.*

VanCleave, Janice. Janice VanCleave's A+ Projects in Biology: Winning Experiments for Science Fairs and Extra Credit. 1993. illus. Wiley, lib. ed., $22.95 (0-471-58629-3); paper, $12.95 (0-471-58628-5).

Gr. 6–10. This volume suggests 30 biology experiments, providing lists of materials, step-by-step directions, interpretation of findings, suggestions for alternative approaches, and ideas for individuals who would like to design their own experiments.

Vogel, Carole Garbuny and **Goldner, Kathryn Allen**. The Great Yellowstone Fire. 1990. illus. Sierra Club; dist. by Little, Brown, $14.95 (0-316-90522-4).

Gr. 4–6. Profusely illustrated with excellent color photographs, this book offers a detailed account of the Yellowstone fires of 1988 and the changing policies regarding forest fires.

Wadsworth, Ginger. Rachel Carson: Voice for the Earth. 1992. illus. Lerner, lib. ed., $21.50 (0-8225-4907-7).

Gr. 5–7. This well-written biography focuses on the life and work of Rachel Carson, the biologist best known as the author of *Silent Spring*. The many black-and-white photographs and illustrations from Carson's books gives the volume an accessible look.

Watts, Barrie. 24 Hours in a Desert. 1991. illus. Watts, lib. ed., $12.90 (0-531-14187-X).

Gr. 3–5. Describing the Sonoran Desert of California, Arizona, and Mexico, this attractive volume focuses on plant and animal life during early morning, daytime, evening, and night. Sharp color photos accompanied by detailed captions add substance to the brief text.

Wood, A. J. Look Again! The Second Ultimate Spot-the-Difference Book. 1992. illus. Dial, $13 (0-8037-0958-7).

Gr. 1–6. What changes occur in plants and animals in a particular environment as the day passes? This book of vivid nature tableaux by Wood and Wilson requires a sharp eye and a curious mind. In each of the 12 double-page spreads, "before" and "after" pictures illuminate habitats from an African jungle to a Florida swamp to polar snowdrifts.

Wu, Norbert. Beneath the Waves: Exploring the Hidden World of the Kelp Forest. 1992. illus. Chronicle, $12.95 (0-87701-835-9).

Gr. 3–7. Exquisite full-color photographs illustrate this informative introduction to the underwater world of the kelp forests located along the coasts of North and South America, southern Africa, and Australia. Wu shares his enthusiasm and extensive knowledge about the forests, noting threats to their existence and describing ecologically sound harvesting practices.

Yolen, Jane. Welcome to the Green House. 1993. illus. Putnam, lib. ed., $14.95 (0-399-22335-5).

K–Gr.3. Dramatic paintings of tropical rain forest flora and fauna will capture children's attention as the steady rhythm of Yolen's brief text evokes the sounds of the "hot green house." This beautiful book makes a quiet plea to protect the environment.

Zoehfeld, Kathleen Weidner. What's Alive? 1995 illus. HarperCollins, $14.95 (0-06-023443-1); lib. ed., $14.89 (0-06-023444-X).

K–Gr.2. Illustrated with cheerful line-and-color illustrations, this book introduces the basic concepts of classification in biology.

Plants

Ardley, Neil. The Science Book of Things That Grow. 1991. illus. Harcourt/Gulliver, $9.95 (0-15-200586-2).

Gr. 1–4. Clear directions and full-color photographs highlight 16 simple projects demonstrating plant growth.

Arnosky, Jim. Crinkleroot's Guide to Knowing the Trees. 1992. illus. Bradbury, $14.95 (0-02-705855-7).

Gr. 1–4. Crinkleroot, a folksy, long-haired woodsman, explains the basic structure, growth, and forms of the trees, as well as how they provide shelter and food for woodland animals. Ink drawings with delicate washes in spring colors combine the lightly comic figure of Crinkleroot with accurate depictions of a variety of forest plants and animals.

Bash, Barbara. Ancient Ones: The World of the Old-Growth Douglas Fir. 1994. illus. Sierra Club; dist. by Little, Brown, $16.95 (0-87156-561-7).

Gr. 3–6. In the Pacific Northwest, a Douglas fir seedling reaches skyward, growing to 300 feet and living, perhaps, for five centuries. Illustrated with watercolor paintings, this beautiful book details the life cycle of the old-growth forest and the variety of wildlife it shelters.

Coil, Suzanne M. Poisonous Plants. 1991. illus. Watts, lib. ed., $11.90 (0-531-20017-5); paper, $5.95 (0-531-15647-8).

Gr. 4–6. Although readers may know the consequences of touching poison ivy, many will be less familiar with the poisonous nature of some common houseplants and of certain wild plants with luscious-looking berries. With precise pen-and-ink and watercolor drawings, this books makes a handy guide.

Cowcher, Helen. Whistling Thorn. 1993. illus. Scholastic, $14.95 (0-590-47299-2).

Gr. 1–3. In a natural history book with narrative appeal, words and watercolor paintings explain a fascinating natural phenomenon: the whistling thorns of Africa's grassland acacia bushes.

Dowden, Anne Ophelia. The Clover & the Bee: A Book of Pollination. 1990. illus. HarperCollins/Crowell, $18 (0-690-04677-4); lib. ed., $17.89 (0-690-04679-0).

Gr. 5–10. Noted botanical illustrator Dowden focuses on pollination, discussing the partnership of flowers and animals as well as other means of plant fertilization. Delicate, precise drawings and paintings appear throughout the book.

Dowden, Anne Ophelia. Poisons in Our Path: Plants That Harm and Heal. 1994. illus. HarperCollins, $17 (0-06-020861-9); lib. ed., $16.89 (0-06-020862-7).

Gr. 4–7. Dowden interweaves botany, history, and folklore in an engaging study of plants important to humankind in magic, lore, and medicine. Through the intriguing text and the many beautiful illustrations, she demonstrates that the beautiful may be deadly and the harmful may also heal.

Ehlert, Lois. Red Leaf, Yellow Leaf. 1991. illus. Harcourt, $14.95 (0-15-266197-2).

K–Gr.3. A child tells of buying, planting, and caring for a sugar maple tree, which becomes a home for animals such as squirrel, a black-capped chickadee, and a downy woodpecker. Bold collages in vivid colors make this an eye-catching picture book.

Frazer, Simon. The Mushroom Hunt. 1995. illus. Candlewick, $14.95 (1-56402-500-4).

Gr. 1–4. From the Read and Wonder series, this picture book tells of a family's hunt for mushrooms and what they discover. Illustrated with shadowy watercolor-and-pencil drawings, it provides an intriguing introduction to mushrooms.

Gibbons, Gail. From Seed to Plant. 1991. illus. Holiday, $15.95 (0-8234-0872-8).

Gr. 1–3. Tracing the cycle of how seeds grow into plants and how flowering plants produce seeds, Gibbons creates a brightly illustrated picture book that includes a simple project (growing beans in a jar) as well as information.

Hiscock, Bruce. The Big Tree. 1991. illus. Atheneum, $14.95 (0-689-31598-8).

Gr. 1–3. Hiscock uses a tree in his neighbor's backyard as the focal point for discussing a tree's life cycle. With a balanced combination of text and colorful paintings, he follows the tree's growth from Revolutionary War days to the present.

Jordan, Helene J. How a Seed Grows. 1992. illus. HarperCollins, $14 (0-06-020104-5); lib. ed., $14.89 (0-06-020185-1); paper, $4.95 (0-06-020185-1).

Gr. 1–2. The revised edition of a Let's-Read-and-Find-Out Science Book, this includes cheerful scenes of children planting seeds and watching them grow, while the text provides simple instructions about what you need to grow daisies or carrots or an oak tree.

Jorgenson, Lisa. Grand Trees of America: Our State and Champion Trees. 1992. illus. Roberts Rinehart, paper, $8.95 (1-879373-15-7).

Gr. 4–7. This large-format paperback describes the official tree of each state, introduces the background and purpose of the National Register of Big Trees, and encourages readers to identify and nominate potential champion trees (the largest of their species). Ink drawings show the overall form of each tree, while smaller close-ups focus on a tree's flowers, leaves, nuts, berries, or cones.

Kelly, M. A. Illus. by **Powzyk, Joyce.** A Child's Book of Wildflowers. 1992. Four Winds, $15.95 (0-02-750142-6).

Gr. 4–7. Introducing 24 North American wildflowers, Powzyk's pencil-and-watercolor artwork lights up the pages with graceful interpretations of the plants in late summer and early fall. The text gives each plant's various common names as well as its botanical name and describes its flowers, stems, and berries.

Kite, Patricia. Insect-Eating Plants. 1995. illus. Millbrook, $15.90 (1-56294-562-9).

Gr. 3–5. This well-written book introduces several types of carnivorous plants and discusses the special adaptations that enable to them to trap and digest insects, as well as the symbiotic relationship they have with bugs and other animals. Colorful photos, spacious design, and fairly large type add visual appeal.

Landau, Elaine. Endangered Plants. 1992. illus. Watts, lib. ed., $12.90 (0-531-20056-6); paper, $5.95 (0-531-15645-1).

Gr. 4–8. Clear full-color photos illustrate this discussion of plants on the verge of extinction. Landau describes a number of plants and explains the reasons why they are endangered and the steps being taken to preserve them.

Landau, Elaine. Wildflowers around the World. 1991. illus. Watts, lib. ed., $12.90 (0-531-20005-1); paper, $5.95 (0-531-15649-4).

Gr. 4–8. Sharp, full-color photos of

flowers from the Arctic tundra and alpine zones, forests, chaparrals, deserts, and tropical and subtropical environments enhance the straightforward text, which includes common and scientific names. Also from the First Book series, Landau's *State Flowers* offers useful information in an easy-to-use format.

Lauber, Patricia. Be a Friend to Trees. 1994. illus. HarperCollins, $15 (0-06-021528-3); lib. ed., $14.89 (0-06-021529-1).

Gr. 2–4. From the Let's-Read-and-Find-Out Science series, this combines simple, informative writing with clear, line-and-watercolor artwork. Lauber talks about trees as home and food for various animals, as providers of fruits and nuts for humans, as sources of wood and paper, and as conservers of soil.

Lavies, Bianca. Mangrove Wilderness: Nature's Nursery. 1994. illus. Dutton, $15.99 (0-525-45186-2).

Gr. 4–6. Lavies' striking photographs accompany her informative, highly readable account of the diverse ecology of a mangrove wilderness.

Lerner, Carol. Cactus. 1992. illus. Morrow, $15 (0-688-09636-0); lib. ed., $14.93 (0-688-09637-9).

Gr. 5–8. Illustrated with Lerner's realistic, detailed artwork, this book introduces the stuctures, habitats, and survival mechanisms of cacti.

Lerner, Carol. Dumb Cane and Daffodils: Poisonous Plants in the House and Garden. 1990. illus. Morrow, $13.95 (0-688-08791-4); lib. ed., $13.88 (0-688-08796-5).

Gr. 5–8. Illustrated with elegant, captioned botanical drawings (most in color), this handsome book discusses domestic plants that grow over wide areas of North America and have a history of poisoning humans.

Lerner, Carol. Plants That Make You Sniffle and Sneeze. 1993. illus. Morrow, $15 (0-688-11489-X); lib. ed., $14.93 (0-688-11490-3).

Gr. 4–6. This intelligent, simply written volume describes plants and pollens that commonly cause hay fever allergies. Botanical illustrations notable for their clarity and grace appear throughout the book, some in full color and others in black and white.

Lucht, Irmgard. The Red Poppy. 1995. illus. Hyperion; dist. by Little, Brown, $13.95 (0-7868-0055-0); lib. ed., $14.89 (0-7868-2043-8).

Gr. 1–3. This striking large-format picture book describes the life cycle of a particular poppy growing at the edge of the field. Colorful, detailed acrylic paintings offer clear and sometimes greatly enlarged views of the poppy and its insect visitors.

Maestro, Betsy. How Do Apples Grow? 1992. illus. HarperCollins, $15 (0-06-020055-3); lib. ed., $14.89 (0-06-020056-1).

Gr. 1–4. From the Let's-Read-and-Find-Out series, this simple, fully illustrated book explains how buds become flowers, which become apples. Deft pastel drawings with watercolor washes show the orchard through the seasons and then zoom in for well-labeled close-ups and cutaway views of flower and fruit.

Maestro, Betsy. Why Do Leaves Change Color? 1994. HarperCollins, $15 (0-06-022873-3); lib. ed., $14.89 (0-06-022874-1).

Gr. 1–4. From the Let's-Read-and-Find-Out Science series, this informative concept book explains what happens to leaves in autumn, as they change colors and then separate from the tree. Bright illustrations show children playing as well as leaves in different sizes, shapes, and colors.

Markle, Sandra. Outside and Inside Trees. 1993. illus. Bradbury, $15.95 (0-02-762313-0).

Gr. 3–5. In this appealing introduction to how trees live and grow, a clear, conversational text describes the structure and function of bark, trunk, roots, leaves, seeds, and pollen. Colorful photographs provide close-up views of the subject.

Mettler, Rene. Flowers. 1993. illus. Scholastic, $10.95 (0-590-46383-7).

K–Gr.2. From the First Discovery Book series, this brightly illustrated little book introduces the structure of flowers, the cycle from budding plant to seed, and the variety of flowers in nature. The occasional transparent pages are used effectively.

Ryder, Joanne. Illus. by **Hays, Michael**. Hello, Tree! 1991. Dutton/Lodestar, $13.95 (0-525-67310-5).

K–Gr.3. Not since Udry's A Tree Is Nice has a mood picture book so effectively portrayed a child's vision of the tree as playground, shelter, friend, and source of mystery. The poetic text finds the right path between fact and imagination, while the handsome, sunlit paintings balance the tree's monumentality with the children's lively humanity. A quiet, sustaining choice for reading aloud.

Tresselt, Alvin. The Gift of the Tree. 1992. illus. Lothrop, $14 (0-688-10684-6); lib. ed., $13.93 (0-688-10685-4).

K–Gr.3. Originally published in 1972 as The Dead Tree, this picture book describes the life, death, and decay of an oak tree in the forest. Even when it's dead, the tree provides food and shelter for many forest creatures, until it finally becomes part of the forest floor from which new oak trees are growing. Beautiful paintings of woodlands stretch across the large, double-page spreads.

Vieira, Linda. The Ever-Living Tree: The Life and Times of a Coast Redwood. 1994. illus. Walker, $14.95 (0-8027-8277-9); lib. ed., $15.85 (0-8027-8278-7).

Gr. 2–5. This nonfiction picture book tells of a redwood tree, from its sprouting until its fall and decay some 2,300 years later. Beautifully textured paintings extend across each double-page spread, showing the forest in the central panel, with images of contemporary events from many cultures in the margins.

Wexler, Jerome. Jack-in-the-Pulpit. 1993. illus. Dutton, $14.99 (0-525-45073-4).

Gr. 3–5. Striking, full-color photographs illustrate Wexler's explanation of the features, structure, habitat, reproduction, and growth stages of this common wildflower.

Wexler, Jerome. Queen Anne's Lace. 1994. illus. Albert Whitman, $14.95 (0-8075-6710-8).

Gr. 3–5. Using text and photographs, Wexler takes a common plant and treats it as completely as one might treat esoteric flora, beginning at the root and continuing to the seed and flowers.

Wexler, Jerome. Sundew Stranglers: Plants That Eat Insects. 1995. illus. Dutton, $15.99 (0-525-45208-7).

Gr. 3–6. Wexler begins with a general introduction to carnivorous or insectivorous plants and then focuses on sundews, beautiful plants whose dewy, sticky leaves are excellent insect catchers. Strikingly composed and intricately detailed, the colorful photographs are both elegant and informative.

Wexler, Jerome. Wonderful Pussy Willows. 1992. illus. Dutton, $14.50 (0-525-44867-5).

Gr. 1–4. Sometimes the best way to

understand general principles of science is by looking closely at specific examples. Here Wexler touches on principles common to many plants, as he discusses the pussy willow. Clear full-color photographs show the plant's form, while the text emphasizes function, examining how the pussy willow grows and how it reproduces through its unusual-looking flowers.

Wiggers, Raymond. Picture Guide to Tree Leaves. 1991. illus. Watts, lib. ed., $11.90 (0-531-20025-6); paper, $5.95 (0-531-15646-X).

Gr. 3–6. Illustrated with color photos of conifers and broad-leafed trees, this volume from the First Book series presents the locations, families, ways of identification, and uses of many species.

Animals

Aaseng, Nathan. Vertebrates. 1993. illus. Watts, lib. ed., $13.40 (0-531-12551-3).

Gr. 5–8. This well-organized book considers the strengths and weaknesses of vertebrates in general, as well as discussing their classes, or subgroups, and some individual species.

Altman, Joyce and **Goldberg, Sue**. Dear Bronx Zoo. 1990. illus. Macmillan, $14.95 (0-02-700640-9); Camelot/Avon, paper, $3.50 (0-380-71649-6).

Gr. 3–6. Culling the most common queries from the Bronx Zoo mailbag, the authors give the questions with answers in general chapters covering mammals, birds, reptiles, primates, nocturnal animals, endangered species, and zoo operations.

Amazing Animals of the World. Ed. by Lawrence T. Lorimer. 24v. 1995. Grolier, $279 (0-7172-7396-2).

Gr. 3–7. Illustrated with a full-color photo and a map, each page in this animal encyclopedia presents one animal: its common and scientific names, classification, length, weight, diet, number of young, and geographical range. A 250-word profile highlights the animal's life cycle and significant features, while symbols indicate its classification, its biome, and (if necessary) its status as endangered or extinct. Student researchers will find this a useful resource.

Arnold, Tim. Natural History from A to Z: A Terrestrial Sampler. 1991. illus. Macmillan/Margaret K. McElderry, $15.95 (0-689-50467-7).

Gr. 4–6. In an eclectic introduction to biology, Arnold discusses one topic beginning with each letter of the alphabet, from *Anteaters* and *Aardvarks* to *Xylem, Yak* and *Zebra Finch*. Along the way, he introduces concepts, such as the Linnean system of classification, continental drift, photosynthesis, and the evolution of species. Handsome black-and-white and color illustrations appear throughout the book.

Arnosky, Jim. Crinkleroot's 25 More Animals Every Child Should Know. 1994. illus. Bradbury, $12.95 (0-02-705846-8).

K–Gr.4. Like Arnosky's Crinkleroot books on fish, birds, and mammals, this cheerful picture guide introduces animals with a simple text and watercolor illustrations. Here emphasis is on creatures not covered in the other books, including a variety of reptiles and insects.

Arnosky, Jim. I See Animals Hiding. 1995. illus. Scholastic, $12.95 (0-590-48143-6).

K–Gr.2. This attractive book, illustrated with watercolor paintings, discusses the ways animals in nature camouflage themselves through their body shapes, protective coloration, and seasonal changes in the fur.

Bare, Colleen Stanley. Who Comes to the Water Hole? 1991. illus. Dutton/Cobblehill, $13.95 (0-525-65073-3).

K–Gr.2. It's the dry season in southern Africa, and many animals, including some unfamiliar ones, find their separate ways to the water hole. The lucid text offers some basic information about each one, while color photos offer views of the changing scene.

Berger, Melvin and **Berger, Gilda**. What Do Animals Do in Winter? How Animals Survive the Cold. 1995. illus. Ideals, lib. ed., $12 (1-57102-055-1); paper, $4.50 (1-57102-041-1).

Gr. 2–4. Clearly written and amply

illustrated in full color, this book discusses animals that migrate, hibernate, hide, or change color in winter.

Bowen, Betsy. Tracks in the Wild. 1993. illus. Little, Brown, $15.95 (0-316-10377-2).

K–Gr.3. Striking woodcut prints tinted with watercolors illustrate the conversational text as Bowen introduces 13 wild animals native to North America and observed near her Minnesota home.

Brimner, Larry Dane. Animals That Hibernate. 1991. illus. Watts, lib. ed., $12.90 (0-531-20018-3).

Gr. 3–5. Illustrated with many full-color photos, this book introduces a series of winter-sleeping creatures and describes their responses to cold. Other books about animals in the First Books series include Brimner's *Unusual Friendships: Symbiosis in the Animal World*, Gutfreund's *Vanishing Animal Neighbors*, Presnall's *Animals That Glow*, and Queri's *Metamorphosis*.

Brooks, Bruce. Making Sense: Animal Perception and Communication. 1993. illus. Farrar, $17 (0-374-34742-5).

Gr. 5–8. Written with flair for the apt analogy, this book examines how animals perceive sensations and communicate with others. Full-color photos appear throughout the book.

Brooks, Bruce. Nature by Design. 1991. illus. Farrar, $13.95 (0-374-30334-7); paper, $8.95 (0-374-35495-2).

Gr. 5–8. Informative and entertaining, this book looks at the precision and ingenuity of animal architecture and discusses animal intelligence.

Brooks, Bruce. Predator! 1991. illus. Farrar, $13.95 (0-374-36111-8); paper, $8.95 (0-374-36112-6).

Gr. 5–8. Written in a witty, conversational style, this book examines the food chain, explaining how and why animals hunt and protect themselves. Brooks also discusses the role of humans as predators, explaining how we have intentionally and sometimes thoughtlessly altered the natural order.

Burnie, David. Communication. 1992. illus. Gloucester; dist. by Watts, lib. ed., $12.40 (0-531-17312-7).

Gr. 4–6. This book provides a concise overview of animal communication by sight, scent, sound, and body movement. Clearly captioned, color photographs and diagrams illustrate the book. Another book in the series is Parker's *Territories*.

Burton, Robert. Illus. by **Burton, Jane**. Egg. 1994. Dorling Kindersley, $13.95 (1-56458-460-7).

Ages 5–8. Beautifully illustrated with excellent, close-up photos and delicate line drawings, this book presents eggs and hatching by looking at 27 animals, mainly birds, that come from eggs.

Collard, Sneed B. Do They Scare You? Creepy Creatures. 1993. illus. Charlesbridge, 85 Main St., Watertown, MA 02172, $14.95 (0-88106-491-2); lib. ed., $15.88 (0-88106-492-0); paper, $6.95 (0-88106-490-4).

Gr. 1–3. Collard presents 22 "scary" animals (vampire bats, piranhas, scorpions) as misunderstood creatures whose only crime is being perfectly suited for their survival. Each creature appears in a full-page or double-page painting with a paragraph or two explaining its unusual looks or behavior.

Craighead, Charles. The Eagle and the River. 1994. illus. Macmillan, $14.95 (0-02-762265-7).

Gr. 2–4. This engaging photo-essay provides a bald eagle's view of Wyoming's Snake River and its wintry surroundings. As the eagle searches for fish, readers learn about the animals and plants in the snow-covered landscape and the twisty, dark blue river.

Curtis, Patricia. Animals and the New Zoos. 1991. illus. Dutton/Lodestar, $15.95 (0-525-67347-4).

Gr. 5–7. Zoos are creating natural and humane habitats for animals previously housed in bare cages. Illustrated with photos, this book discusses the lifestyles of many animals in the context of how zoos are learning to care for them.

Dewey, Jennifer Owings. Animal Architecture. 1991. illus. Watts/Orchard, $14.95 (0-531-05930-8); lib. ed., $14.99(0-531-08530-9).

Gr. 4–6. Writing in a genial, conversational tone, Dewey introduces more than a dozen animal architects, shows how and why they build things, and, along the way, teaches a good deal about their lives. Softly shaded pencil drawings illustrate this handsome book.

Dorros, Arthur. Animal Tracks. 1991. illus. Scholastic, $13.95 (0-590-43367-9).

K–Gr.3. Dorros shows the marks left by 22 animals and invites readers to identify who's been walking where. This attractive book promises to engage young naturalists.

Doubilet, Anne. Illus. by **Doubilet, David.** Under the Sea from A to Z. 1991. Crown, $16 (0-517-57836-0); lib. ed., $16.99 (0-517-57837-9).

Gr. 3–7. Much like a magazine in design, this large-format book features one brilliantly colored photograph on each page along with a paragraph of information about a sea-dwelling animal.

Downer, Ann. Don't Blink Now! Capturing the Hidden World of Sea Creatures. 1991. illus. Watts, $14.90 (0-531-15225-1); lib. ed., $13.90 (0-531-11072-9).

Gr. 4–8. Action photographs in glowing color illustrate this introduction to ocean animals. The chatty text discusses topics such as survival, reproduction, and the hunt for food.

Dykstra, Mary. The Amateur Zoologist: Explorations and Investigations. 1994. illus. Watts, lib. ed., $12.90 (0-531-11162-8).

Gr. 6–9. Dykstra outlines the scientific methods and some sensible guidelines for studying animals, then offers ideas and procedures for field studies and science projects of animals such as earthworms, sowbugs, hydras, and gerbils. Another book in the series is Roth's *The Amateur Naturalist.*

Endangered Wildlife of the World. 11v. 1993. Marshall Cavendish, $399.95 (1-85435-489-2).

Gr. 4–10. This 11-volume set includes 1,200 species and subspecies of amphibians, birds, fish, insects, invertebrates, mammals, and reptiles considered endangered, threatened, or vulnerable. Each one- to three-page entry includes scientific name and classification as well as a description of its diet, reproduction, behavior, appearance, habitat, the reason for its decline, and the strategies for its survival. Most entries include a color photo or black-and-white drawing of the animal as well as a range map. Students will find this an attractive and easy-to-use resource.

Evans, Lisa Gollin. An Elephant Never Forgets Its Snorkel: How Animals Survive without Tools and Gadgets. 1992. illus. Crown, $10 (0-517-58401-8); lib. ed., $10.99 (0-517-58404-2).

Gr. 3–5. Illustrated with watercolors, this entertaining volume presents 18 analogies showing how human inventions mimic animals' physical adaptations and behavior. For example, elephants use their trunks as we use snorkels and African termites build 20-foot-tall dirt structures complete with single-purpose rooms and ventilation ducts, just as we build highrises.

Facklam, Margery. And Then There Was One: The Mysteries of Extinction. 1990. illus. Sierra Club; dist. by Little, Brown, $14.95 (0-316-25984-5); paper, $5.95 (0-87156-573-0).

Gr. 3–5. Facklam discusses the natural forces causing a species to die out, as well as humankind's responsibility for destroying habitats and causing a quickening pace of extinction in recent times. Soft, shaded pencil drawings complement the text of this handsome book.

Facklam, Margery. Bees Dance and Whales Sing: The Mysteries of Animal Communication. 1992. illus. Sierra Club; dist. by Little, Brown, lib. ed., $14.95 (0-87156-573-0).

Gr. 4–6. How can a flock of 10,000 starlings make a quick turn together and never crash into one another? Facklam uses specific examples to discuss animal communication, explaining technical information with clarity and a sense of wonder. The unanswered questions are as fascinating as the amazing facts.

Few, Roger. Macmillan Children's Guide to Endangered Animals. 1993. illus. Macmillan, $17.95 (0-02-734545-9).

Gr. 5–8. Few organizes his material according to habitats, describing each endangered animal in one or two paragraphs illustrated by a colorful photograph or painting.

Fichter, George S. Poisonous Animals. 1991. illus. Watts, lib. ed., $12.90 (0-531-20050-7).

Gr. 3–5. Illustrated with unusually sharp color photographs, this clearly written book discusses animals such as cobras, black widows, and wasps. Fichter emphasizes that they use their venom in self-defense and would generally prefer to escape rather than to attack.

Flegg, Jim and others. Animal Builders. 1991. illus. Newington, lib. ed., $10.90 (1-878137-05-0).

Gr. 4–7. Clearly written and illustrated with photographs, this book presents several kinds of nest-building birds, papermaking wasps, web- and trap-spinning spiders, and tunnel-digging mammals. Other volumes in the series include *Animal Communication, Animal Families, Animal Helpers, Animal Hunters, Animal Movement, Animal Senses,* and *Animal Travelers.*

Gelman, Rita Golden. Dawn to Dusk in the Galápagos: Flightless Birds, Swimming Lizards, and Other Fascinating Creatures. 1991. illus. Little, Brown, $16.95 (0-316-30739-4).

Gr. 5–7. Illustrated with many large, beautiful photos, this book concisely explains the Galápagos' volcanic origins, then describes a typical day and night for the islands' wildlife. Gelman's clear, vivid prose underscores how the animals' behavior and physical characteristics have evolved in response to the harsh conditions of Galápagos life.

Goodman, Billy. Animal Homes and Societies. 1992. illus. Little, Brown, $17.95 (0-316-32018-8).

Gr. 4–8. This large-format book is divided into four sections: "Living Alone," "Close Families," "Extended Families," and "Large Groups." Within each section, Goodman focuses on a few well-chosen examples and discusses the intriguing details of their social behavior. Colorful photos provide close-up views of the animals discussed.

The Grolier Student Encyclopedia of Endangered Species. Ed. by Diane Chando Frenick. 10v. 1995. Grolier, $279 (0-7172-7385-7).

Gr. 4–8. This useful encyclopedia includes 400 animals organized alphabetically by common name. Each entry is about a page long and includes a large color photo of the animal in its habitat as well as a description of the animal, its size, habitat, diet, breeding habits, and young. It also notes the estimated remaining populations, the reasons for endangerment, and whether any conservation measures are being employed.

Guiberson, Brenda. Spoonbill Swamp. 1992. illus. Holt, $14.95 (0-8050-1583-3); paper, $4.95 (0-8050-3385-8).

Gr. 1–3. This simple science picture book follows a day in the lives of a spoonbill mother and an alligator mother in a southern swamp. Watercolor paintings capture the setting, while vivid narration brings the animals, the action, and the habitat to life.

Hirschi, Ron. Dance with Me. 1995. Dutton/Cobblehill, $14.99 (0-525-65204-3).

Gr. 2–4. With clear photographs showing the flapping, leaping, soaring, and splashing animal behaviors that people might call dancing, Hirschi explains the way such motions are used in animal courtship, greeting, bonding, or defense.

Hirschi, Ron. Illus. by **Cox, Daniel J.** Loon Lake. 1991. Dutton/Cobblehill, $13.95 (0-525-65046-6).

K–Gr.2. Paddle with me quietly, slowly, invites Hirschi at the beginning of this photo-tour of a northern lake. In the following pages, children travel the lake's reedy shore to meet waterfowl, turtles, deer, frogs, and other wildlife in their natural habitats. Half the book is devoted to the loon. Large type, clean design, and striking photos give the book great visual appeal.

Hirschi, Ron. Mountain. 1992. illus. Bantam/Little Rooster, $13 (0-553-07998-0); paper, $4.99 (0-553-35495-7).

Ages 5–8. This attractive picture book uses watercolor artwork and a simple, find-the-animal text to introduce animals

living in mountain regions. Like Hirschi's *Desert*, also from the Discover My World series, this is an appealing resource for young children studying habitats.

Hirschi, Ron. A Time for Playing. 1994. illus. Dutton, $13.99 (0-525-65159-4).

K–Gr.2. Hirschi describes animals at play: the dances of polar bears, the grooming of sea otters, and the quicksilver antics of chipmunks. This handsome book features a generous layout, large type, and spectacular color photographs. Others in the series include *A Time for Babies* and *A Time for Sleeping*.

The Illustrated Encyclopedia of Wildlife. 15v. 1991. Grey Castle; dist. by Encyclopaedia Britannica, $495 (0-55905-052-7).

Gr. 5–10. Excellent, full-color photos, paintings, and maps illustrate this wildlife encyclopedia, which covers single-cell animals as well as more complex creatures. Arranged according to scientific classification, the articles discuss broad families of animals, then focus on some individual species.

Johnson, Jinny. Skeletons: An Inside Look at Animals. 1994. illus. Reader's Digest; dist. by Random, $16.95 (0-89577-604-9).

Gr. 3–7. Black pages form a dramatic backdrop for this striking oversize book. Each double-page spread features the skeleton of a different animal, accompanied by text and captions. The excellent full-color illustrations of the animals and their skeletons give the book browsing appeal; it also offers a good beginning lesson in comparative anatomy and a great deal of miscellaneous information about animal behavior.

Kaufman, Les and others. Alligators to Zooplankton: A Dictionary of Water Babies. 1991. illus. Watts, lib. ed., $15.90 (0-531-10995-X).

Gr. 4–7. This appealing New England

Aquarium book introduces baby marine animals (including eels, octopi, and whales) and discusses how they are cared for and how they look, compared with older animals. Spectacular color photography and a lively text will draw readers to this appealing book.

Kingfisher Illustrated Encyclopedia of Animals: From Aardvark to Zorille—and 2,000 Other Animals. Ed. by Michael Chinery. 1992. illus. Kingfisher, $19.95 (1-85697-801-X).

Gr. 4–6. Each concise entry describes the animal, its behavior, geographic range, and habitat, as well as its order, family, and species. Color drawings and photos illustrate many of the entries. A useful index concludes the volume.

Kitchen, Bert. And So They Build. 1993. illus. Candlewick, $15.95 (1-56402-217-X).

Gr. 2–4. Kitchen provides exquisitely detailed portraits of 12 animals and what they build. On the page facing each illustration is a paragraph or two on the animal's habits and the process of making its unique construction. Using the same format, Kitchen's *When Hunger Calls* explores the ingenious ways used by 12 different animals to obtain food.

Kudlinski, Kathleen V. Animal Tracks and Traces. 1991. illus. Watts, $12.95 (0-531-15185-9); lib. ed., $12.90 (0-531-10742-6).

Gr. 3–5. Pleasant watercolor illustrations enhance this clear guide to tracking animals, especially urban and suburban beasts such as squirrels, mice, and sparrows. Every chapter includes information on animal behavior, as well as simple activities and a puzzle.

Lacey, Elizabeth A. What's the Difference? A Guide to Some Familiar Animal Look-alikes. 1993. illus. Clarion, $14.95 (0-395-56182-5).

Gr. 4–6. This informative book focuses on the similarities and differences between seven animal pairs, including alligator and crocodile, tortoise and turtle, and camel and dromedary. Dramatic cross-hatched drawings illustrate the text.

Lambert, David. The Children's Animal Atlas: How Animals Have Evolved, Where They Live Today, Why So Many Are in Danger. 1992. illus. Millbrook, lib. ed., $18.90 (1-56294-167-4).

Gr. 4–8. With double-page spreads featuring particular habitats, this atlas introduces the animal life of the region, describes each animal, and illustrates it with a photograph. Drawings and charts depict information such as the formation of atolls and the structure of a termite nest. This atlas includes water environments such as rivers, salt marshes, and frozen oceans.

Lasky, Kathryn. Illus. by **Knight, Christopher G.** and **Swedberg, Jack.** Think like an Eagle: At Work with a Wildlife Photographer. 1992. Little, Brown/Joy Street, $15.95 (0-316-51519-1).

Gr. 3–7. Lasky and Knight follow wildlife photographer Jack Swedberg across the U.S. as he takes pictures of eagles in Massachusetts, alligators in Florida, and humpback whales off the coast of Alaska. The text discusses Swedborg's techniques, including the use of blinds (camouflaged structures), while the many full-color photos make this volume a visual delight.

Lauber, Patricia. Fur, Feathers, and Flippers: How Animals Live Where They Do. 1994. illus. Scholastic, $16.95 (0-590-45071-9).

Gr. 4–8. With amazing color photographs and a precise, factual text, Lauber's beautiful photo-essay offers vivid examples of how the plants and animals "fit together" to help each other survive. In separate chapters, she looks at five widely differing habitats: the seas of Antarctica, the grasslands of East Africa, the forests of New England, the desert of the southwestern U.S., and the tundra of the Far North.

Machotka, Hana. Terrific Tails. 1994. illus. Morrow, $15 (0-688-04562-6).

Ages 5–8. Illustrated with full-color photos, this informative book has an intriguing guess-and-learn format that provides close-up views of seven different types of animal tails and explains how each helps its owner survive. Other titles in this excellent series include *Breathtaking Noses, Outstanding Outsides, What Do You Do at a Petting Zoo?* and *What Neat Feet.*

Marshall Cavendish International Wildlife Encyclopedia. Rev. ed. 25v. 1990. Marshall Cavendish, $499.99 (0-86307-734X).

Gr. 5–10. Each informative article in this 25-volume encyclopedia includes the animal's scientific classification and at least one illustration. Most articles extend for more than a page and include photos in color as well as in black and white. Though the print is rather small, the alphabetical arrangement by common name of animal and the broad coverage make this a favorite resource for reports.

Martin, James. Hiding Out. 1993. illus. Crown, $13 (0-517-59392-0); paper, $13.99 (0-517-59393-9).

Gr. 2–4. A clearly written text and wonderfully sharp photos distinguish this book describing the ways in which animals disguise themselves to blend with their environments for protection or to help them prey upon others.

Matthews, Downs. Arctic Summer. 1993. illus. Simon & Schuster, $14 (0-671-79539-2).

Gr. 4–6. This book eloquently describes the brief Arctic summer. Good color photographs record the ani-

mals, hunting and hunted, as well as the blooming plants, startling in their unexpected brilliance.

Maynard, Christopher. Amazing Animal Facts. 1993. illus. Knopf, $18 (0-679-85085-6).

Gr. 3–7. With crisp-edged color photos and drawings, this visually appealing book devotes double-page spreads to 26 animals, ranging from bats to beetles to sharks. Each lead question (for example, "Is a wolf a dog?") is followed by other related questions ("Can wolves sing?") about the topic.

Maynard, Thane. Animal Olympians: The Fastest, Strongest, Toughest, and Other Wildlife Champions. 1994. illus. Watts, lib. ed., $15.90 (0-531-11159-8).

Gr. 4–6. Conservationist Maynard combines substance with entertaining trivia to keep children turning the pages. Colorful photographs appear on nearly every page.

McClung, Robert M. Lost Wild America: The Story of Our Extinct and Vanishing Wildlife. Rev. ed. 1993. Shoe String, $25 (0-208-02359-3).

Gr. 5–8. This useful, readable book gives readers the checkered story of American wildlife management from pioneer days to the present. A good resource for reports on extinct and endangered animals, it includes examples of vanished species as well as those coming back from the brink of extinction and others whose survival is still an open question.

McGovern, Ann and **Clark, Eugenie**. The Desert beneath the Sea. 1991. illus. Scholastic, $13.95 (0-590-42638-9).

K–Gr.3. Writer McGovern and marine biologist Clark describe the wondrous creatures they studied during scuba-diving forays—an octopus with horns and lionfish with poison-tipped dorsal fins.

Mullins, Patricia. V for Vanishing: An Alphabet of Endangered Animals. 1994. illus. HarperCollins, $15 (0-06-023556-X); lib. ed., $14.89 (0-06-023557-8).

K–Gr.2. Offering a good mix of well-publicized and lesser-known animals, this alphabet book provides information and exquisite collage illustrations for 25 endangered animals.

Paladino, Catherine. Our Vanishing Farm Animals. 1991. illus. Little, Brown/Joy Street, $15.95 (0-316-68891-6).

Gr. 4–6. Handsome, well-chosen color photographs illustrate Paladino's informative discussion of endangered farm animals, which are often ignored in the broader topic of vanishing species. In clear, informative prose she introduces the eight breeds of farm animals that have fallen out of fashion and face the possibility of extinction.

Parker, Steve. Inside the Whale and Other Animals. 1992. illus. Doubleday, $16 (0-385-30651-2).

Gr. 4–8. With cutaway views showing cross sections of animals' systems, the line-and-watercolor artwork takes center stage here, though the succinct paragraphs of text are surprisingly informative. Smaller drawings illustrate the details—the hinged jaw of a rattlesnake, the unique digestive system of a starfish.

Parker, Steve. Natural World. 1994. illus. Dorling Kindersley, $29.95 (1-56458-719-3).

Gr. 6–12. Lavishly illustrated in glowing color, this large-size volume in the Eyewitness Natural World series provides dazzling photos, clear diagrams, and lively text. With double-page spreads on topics such as animal anatomy, feeding, life cycles, evolution, and habitat, this approach popularizes zoology without oversimplification.

Patent, Dorothy Hinshaw. Illus. by **Muñoz, William.** What Good Is a Tail? 1994. Dutton/Cobblehill, $13.99 (0-525-65148-9).

Gr. 2–5. Patent answers the title question and more in this short, appealing book, illustrated with excellent color photographs.

Pollock, Steve. The Atlas of Endangered Animals. 1993. illus. Facts On File, $17.95 (0-8160-2856-7).

Gr. 5–8. This atlas takes a regional approach to presenting endangered animals. Color photographs illustrate the animals discussed, while maps indicate their geographical range.

Powzyk, Joyce. Animal Camouflage: A Closer Look. 1990. illus. Bradbury, $15.95 (0-02-774980-0).

Gr. 2–5. Powzyk explains the different sorts of animal camouflage and provides an album of examples of each type of disguise. The watercolor and colored-pencil illustrations show how easily the animals blend in with their surroundings.

Rauzon, Mark J. Feet, Flippers, Hooves, and Hands. 1994. illus. Lothrop, $13 (0-688-10234-4).

K–Gr.2. A brief text accompanies the clear, colorful photos looking at the hands, feet, and flippers of various animals. Useful in primary-grade classrooms, other books in the series include *Eyes and Ears, Skin, Scales, Feathers, and Fur* and *Horns, Antlers, Fangs, and Tusks.*

Roop, Peter and **Roop, Connie.** One Earth, a Multitude of Creatures. 1992. Walker, $14.95 (0-8027-8192-6); lib. ed., $15.85 (0-8027-8193-4).

K–Gr.2. Attractive paintings show the Pacific Northwest ecosystem in this gentle introduction to the interdependence and diversity of animals in an environment. A simple caption describes each scene and includes the group name for that particular creature (an "unkindness" of ravens, for example).

Rosen, Michael J. All Eyes on the Pond. 1994. illus. Hyperion; dist. by Little, Brown, $14.95 (1-56282-475-9); lib. ed., $14.89 (1-56282-476-7).

K–Gr.2. Rhymed couplets accompany acrylic paintings focusing on animals of the pond, from water strider to turtle to bluegill. Young children will find this a good visual introduction to pond life.

Ruiz, Andres Llamas. Animals on the Inside: A Book of Discovery & Learning. 1995. illus. Sterling, $17.95 (0-8069-0830-0).

Gr. 3–6. Each double-page spread in this brightly illustrated book focuses on a different animal, with a large painting showing the creature inside and out, labels and captions commenting on various parts of its body, and several paragraphs of text commenting on its special features.

Ryder, Joanne.Dancers in the Garden. 1992. illus. Sierra Club; dist. by Little, Brown, lib. ed., $15.95 (0-87156-578-1).

Ages 5–8. Delicate watercolors illustrate this book about hummingbirds dancing through their day in a Japanese garden, while Ryder's precise, poetic prose leads the reader through the birds' natural cycle.

Sargent, William. Night Reef: Dusk to Dawn on a Coral Reef. 1991. illus. Watts, $14.95 (0-531-15219-7); lib. ed., $14.90 (0-531-11073-7).

Gr. 4–7. Using examples from the Caribbean, the Red Sea, and the Pacific Ocean, Sargent examines the wide range of nocturnal life that inhabits a coral reef and the lagoon within it. Vivid descriptions and spectacular underwater photographs brighten this informative book.

Sinclair, Sandra. Extraordinary Eyes: How Animals See the World. 1992. illus. Dial, $15 (0-8037-0803-3); lib. ed., $14.89 (0-8037-0806-8).

Gr. 5–8. Loaded with sharp, full-color photographs, many of them close-ups, this intriguing book takes a comparative approach to the study of animal sight organs.

Taylor, Barbara . The Animal Atlas. 1992. illus. Knopf, $20 (0-679-80501-X); lib. ed., $21.99 (0-679-90501-4).

Gr. 3–7. Each double-page spread depicts the animal life of one region on the earth, with a map of the area and a smaller locator map showing it on the hemisphere. An introduction describes the area, then each animal is named (including scientific name), described, and portrayed in an attractive color illustration.

Taylor, Dave. Endangered Grassland Animals. 1992. illus. Crabtree, lib. ed., $15.95 (0-86505-528-9); paper, $7.95 (0-86505-538-6).

Gr. 3–5. Fully illustrated with excellent color photographs, this volume introduces readers to 10 species living in the grasslands of Africa, Australia, and North America. Brief discussions of grassland ecology and preservation begin and end the book. Other books in the series include *Endangered Forest Animals*, *Endangered Mountain Animals*, and *Endangered Wetland Animals*.

Wildlife of the World. 13v. 1994. Marshall Cavendish, $289.95 (1-85435-592-9).

Gr. 4–7. This encyclopedia offers two- to four-page articles on more than

300 animals: mammals, birds, reptiles, amphibians, fish, and invertebrates. Each article includes the animal's common and scientific names, appearance, habits, food, reproduction, habitat, range, and status (from extinct to widespread). A map indicates distribution, and two color photos show the animal in its natural habitat. This set offers a good overview of a variety of animals.

Wolkomir, Joyce Rogers and **Wolkomir, Richard**. Junkyard Bandicoots and Other Tales of the World's Endangered Species. 1992. illus. Wiley, paper, $9.95 (0-471-57261-6).

Gr. 4–6. This book highlights more than 35 of the world's endangered species, detailing how they live, why they are disappearing, and what can be done to save them. Additional sections explain how prairies, rain forests, old-growth forests, seashores, and woodland streams support a great variety of flora and fauna.

World Wildlife Habitats. 3v. 1992. illus. Marshall Cavendish, $139.95 (1-85435-433-7).

A companion set to the *Marshall Cavendish International Wildlife Encyclopedia*, this discusses 23 different habitats, ranging from tropical rain forests to towns and cities. Each clearly written chapter discusses a separate habitat, including its topography, climate, seasonal changes, plant and animal life, and conservation. Many attractive color photographs, line drawings, and charts illustrate the text.

Lower Animals

Aaseng, Nathan. Invertebrates. 1993. illus. Watts, lib. ed., $13.40 (0-531-12550-5).

Gr. 5–9. This well-organized book discusses species of invertebrates and explains why some animals that appear dissimilar may be grouped together in scientific classification.

Bernhard, Emery. Dragonfly. 1993. illus. Holiday, $15.95 (0-8234-1033-1).

Gr. 1–3. In this illustrated book, a dragonfly winging its way across a backdrop of blue, clouded sky leads readers from page to page to discover facts about dragonfly morphology, behavior, mating, and maturation, and a little about dragonflies in culture and myth. The approach is direct, yet the writing is colorful and includes plenty of enlivening details.

Bernhard, Emery. Ladybug. 1992. illus. Holiday, $14.95 (0-8234-0986-4).

Gr. 1–3. This colorful book combines scientific fact with descriptive, appealing paintings to introduce and explore the life cycle of the ladybug.

Bodecker, N. M. Illus. by **Blegvad, Erik**. Water Pennies and Other Poems. 1991. Macmillan/Margaret K. McElderry, $12.95 (0-689-50517-5).

K–Gr.3. These delicate poems evoke the fragility and the sturdiness of insects and small creatures. Blegvad's realistic ink drawings enhance the wordplay and the sense of hesitancy and drift.

Brenner, Barbara and **Chardiet, Bernice**. Where's That Insect? 1993. illus. Scholastic, $10.95 (0-590-45210-X).

Gr. 2–4. With the aid of an agreeable text and small, detailed watercolor illustrations, the reader learns some simple facts about 14 insects. Larger, more lavish "hide & seek" paintings allow children to locate the featured insects in their appropriate ecosystems.

Cerullo, Mary M. Lobsters: Gangsters of the Sea. 1994. illus. Dutton, $15.99 (0-525-65153-5).

Gr. 4–6. With fine color pictures and an informative text, this lively photo-essay captures the behavior of lobsters and their relationship with the people who catch them.

Chinery, Michael. Spider. 1990. illus. Troll Associates, lib. ed., $11.59 (0-8167-2108-4); paper, $3.95 (0-8167-2109-2).

Gr. 2–5. The Life Story series, which includes Chinery's *Ant* and *Butterfly*, presents the appearance and physical features of each animal at various stages of its life cycle, in addition to giving more general information about its behavior. Exceptionally clear, close-up photographs offer remarkable views of subjects such as a butterfly's egg.

Demuth, Patricia. Illus. by **Schindler, S. D**. Those Amazing Ants. 1994. Macmillan, $14.95 (0-02-728467-0).

K–Gr.2. Schindler's sensitive artwork takes viewers up close for good views of ants on the ground and in their tunnels, while Demuth tells the amazing details of ant behavior.

Dewey, Jennifer Owings. Spiders Near and Far. 1993. illus. Dutton, lib. ed., $14.99 (0-525-44979-5).

Gr. 4–7. Dewey's handsome, colored-pencil illustrations and clear, informative text will add to kids' knowledge without diminishing their shivery fascination with spiders. The final double-page spread shows several particular spiders drawn life-size.

Esbensen, Barbara Juster. Sponges Are Skeletons. 1993. illus. HarperCollins, $15 (0-06-021034-6); lib. ed., $14.89 (0-06-021037-0).

Gr. 1–4. From the Let's-Read-and-Find-Out series, this book explains that some bath sponges are actually the skeletons of animals that have been harvested by divers from the ocean floor. Lively illustrations animate the simple, thought-provoking text.

Facklam, Margery. The Big Bug Book. 1994. illus. Little, Brown, $15.95 (0-316-27389-9).

Gr. 1–3. This intriguing book introduces 13 insects of impressive size, illustrated in amazingly realistic, air-brushed paintings. Each double-page spread features a realistic, full-size picture of a bug in a setting that makes its size apparent, while the text describes its features and habits.

French, Vivian. Illus. by **Voake, Charlotte**. Caterpillar Caterpillar. 1993. Candlewick, $14.95 (1-56402-206-4).

Ages 4–8. As a little girl watches caterpillars growing, she learns firsthand about their development. This captivating picture book conveys information and a love of nature through the first-person narrative and the equally pleasing and ingenuous ink-and-watercolor artwork.

Gaffney, Michael. Secret Forests. 1994. illus. Western/Artists & Writers Guild, $14.95 (0-307-17505-7).

Gr. 1–5. This large-format introduction to tiny animals features realistic paintings of the canopy and the floor of a tropical forest, oak leaves, leaf litter, and the bark and floor of a pine forest. These scenes challenge readers to find the animals, which have blended into the scenery of their habitats. Other

pages show the individual animals clearly and tell a little about each one.

Gibbons, Gail. Spiders. 1993. illus. Holiday, lib. ed., $15.95 (0-8234-1006-4); paper, $5.95 (0-8234-1081-1).

K–Gr.2. In simple prose, Gibbons describes physical characteristics, behavior, habitats, and several distinctive species. Bright line-and-watercolor artwork illustrates this attractive introduction to spiders.

Goor, Ron and **Goor, Nancy**. Insect Metamorphosis. 1990. illus. Simon & Schuster/Atheneum, $14.95 (0-689-31445-0).

Gr. 2–5. Exceptionally sharp, colorful close-ups illustrate this book, which presents a series of insects and clearly explains the changes they go through as they mature.

Gowell, Elizabeth Tayntor. Sea Jellies: Rainbows in the Sea. 1993. illus. Watts, $15.95 (0-531-15259-6); lib. ed., $15.90 (0-531-11152-0).

Gr. 1–4. Excellent color photographs illustrate this in-depth study of jellies, some of the simplest animals alive. Well-labeled color diagrams expand the informative text.

Hopf, Alice L. Spiders. 1990. illus. Dutton/Cobblehill, $13.95 (0-525-65017-2).

Gr. 4–7. Colorful, close-up photos illustrate this discussion of what spiders are, what they do, and how they differ from one another.

Kite, Patricia. Down in the Sea: The Octopus. 1993. illus. Albert Whitman, lib. ed., $13.95 (0-8075-1715-1).

Gr. 1–3. With eye-catching color photographs and simple, concise writing, this book introduces the octopus, its physical characteristics, life cycle, and eating habits. Other volumes in the series explore the jellyfish, the sea slug, and the crab.

LaBonte, Gail. Leeches, Lampreys, and Other Cold-Blooded Bloodsuckers. 1991. illus. Watts, lib. ed., $12.90 (0-531-20027-2).

Gr. 3–6. Lively writing and full-color photographs add to the appeal of this book on bloodsuckers, parasites that get the protein they need from the blood of other animals.

Lasky, Kathryn. Monarchs. 1993. illus. Harcourt, $16.95 (0-15-255296-0); paper, $8.95 (0-15-255297-9).

Gr. 4–6. Lasky offers biological information and a sense of the miracle of the migrating monarch butterfly in eminently readable prose. Detailed color photographs and the personal stories make the discussion more even more engaging.

Lauber, Patricia. Earthworms: Underground Farmers. 1994. illus. Holt, $14.95 (0-8050-1910-3).

Gr. 3–6. Lauber introduces the anatomy, physiology, and life cycle of worms as well as their habitat and the role they play in aerating the soil and decomposing waste. Short chapters, large print, and several full-color photos make for an attractive layout that will appeal to young readers.

Lauber, Patricia. Illus. by **Keller, Holly**. An Octopus Is Amazing. 1990. Harper-Collins/Crowell, $15.95 (0-690-04801-7); lib. ed., $14.89 (0-690-04803-3).

Gr. 1–3. Illustrated with clear, colorful artwork, this Let's-Read-and-Find-Out book introduces young readers to the octopus. The simple text describes the animal's physical features and explains some of its more fascinating capabilities.

Lavies, Bianca. Backyard Hunter: The Praying Mantis. 1990. illus. Dutton, $13.95 (0-525-44547-1).

K–Gr.4. Beginning with an amazing photo of a hatching egg case, Lavies describes the stages of this insect's life and discusses some of its unusual characteristics. This beautifully designed photo-essay is both stunning to look at and fascinating to read.

Lavies, Bianca. Compost Critters. 1993. illus. Dutton, $14.99 (0-525-44763-6).

Gr. 3–5. Close-up photographs discover mystery and even beauty in such low-life sights of the compost heap as bread mold and rotting tomatoes, while the magnifying lens of the camera transforms nematodes, mites, and sow bugs into magnificent monsters. Accurate, well organized, and informative, this intriguing book tells of new life growing from old, of garbage turning into rich humus.

Lavies, Bianca. Monarch Butterflies: Mysterious Travelers. 1992. illus. Dutton, lib. ed., $14.99 (0-525-44905-1).

Gr. 4–7. Lavies traveled to Mexico's Sierra Madre to photograph a secluded butterfly migration site, the winter home of monarchs that summer in the eastern U.S. and Canada. Illustrated with captivating, full-color photographs, this book introduces the behavior and life stages of the monarch butterfly.

Lavies, Bianca. Wasps at Home. 1991. illus. Dutton, $13.95 (0-525-44704-0).

Gr. 2–5. This attractive book clearly describes the home life of the social wasp: how the queen builds her colony, how the workers develop from eggs to adults, how work is divided within the nest, and how the colony's life comes to a close at the end of summer. The large photos seem to bring the reader right inside the nest. Similar in format and visual impact is Lavies' *Killer Bees*.

Markle, Sandra. Outside and Inside Spiders. 1994. illus. Bradbury, $15.95 (0-02-762314-9).

Gr. 4–6. Markle first distinguishes spiders from insects, then explains their habitats, lifestyles, and mating. As the series name implies, this book features the spider's internal structure as well as its visible features. Large color photographs accompany the text.

Martin, James. Tentacles: The Amazing World of Octopus, Squid, and Their Relatives. 1993. illus. Crown, $14 (0-517-59149); lib. ed., $14.99 (0-517-59150-2).

Gr. 3–6. Illustrated with spectacular color photos, this book describes sea creatures such as the nautilus, the octopus, the squid, and the cuttlefish. Each animal is spotlighted in a separate chapter detailing its structure, feeding patterns, reproductive capabilities, and special abilities.

Meyers, Susan. Illus. by **Hewett, Richard.** Insect Zoo. 1991. Dutton/Lodestar, $16.95 (0-525-67325-3).

Gr. 4–6. This engaging book introduces the San Francisco Insect Zoo, where visitors have the chance to stroke a tarantula, smell stinkbugs, and peek inside a termite nest. Many large, clear photos illustrate the cogent text.

Richardson, Joy. Illus. by **Owen, Angela.** Mollusks. 1993. Watts, lib. ed., $11.40 (0-531-14263-9).

K–Gr.2. Richardson introduces snails, slugs, limpets, octopuses, and other mollusks. Like other books in the Picture Science series, including *Fish*, *Flowers*, and *Reptiles*, this offers basic information in large type with a full-color, close-up photo on every other page.

Ryder, Joanne. Illus. by **Stock, Catherine.** When the Woods Hum. 1991. Morrow, $13.95 (0-688-07057-4); lib. ed., $13.88 (0-688-07058-2).

K–Gr.3. Illustrated with delicate watercolor artwork, this picture book tells the story of several generations of a family observing cicadas in the same woods. Though fictional, it provides solid information on the life cycle of periodical cicadas.

Snedden, Robert. What Is an Insect?. 1993. illus. Sierra Club; dist. by Little, Brown, $13.95 (0-87156-540-4).

Gr. 2–5. Striking full-color photographs combined with detailed color drawings highlight succinct discussion of the physical characteristics, life cycles, and behaviors of insects.

Souza, D. M. Insects around the House. 1991. illus. Carolrhoda, lib. ed., $17.50 (0-87614-438-5).

Gr. 3–5. Attractive color photographs, some so clear that the creatures seem ready to crawl off the pages, brighten this book on familiar insects from the Creatures All around Us series, which also includes *Eight Legs*, *What Bit Me?* and *Insects in the Garden*.

Fish

Aliki. My Visit to the Aquarium. 1993. illus. HarperCollins, $15 (0-06-021458-9); lib. ed., $14.89 (0-06-021459-7).

Ages 5–8. A young boy takes readers on a tour of the aquarium. Each fish described in the boy's narration is identified in an illustration by clear, unobtrusive script. The dominant blues and greens of Aliki's watercolors provide visual continuity amid the riot of brightly colored fish.

Arnold, Caroline. Illus. by **Hewett, Richard**. Watch Out for Sharks! 1991. Clarion, $15.45 (0-395-57560-5).

Gr. 2–5. Excellent color photographs show models of gaping shark mouths filled with razor-sharp teeth. While Arnold's focus is on the appearance and physiology of a variety of sharks, she also discusses popular myths, evolution, related fish, habitats, possible extinction, and shark scholarship.

Arnosky, Jim. Crinkleroot's 25 Fish Every Child Should Know. 1993. illus. Bradbury, paper, $12.95 (0-02-705844-1).

K–Gr.4. Folksy woodsman Crinkleroot is back to help young naturalists learn to identify common types of fish. Line-and-watercolor illustrations brighten the pages of this introductory guidebook.

Cerullo, Mary M. Sharks: Challengers of the Deep. 1993. illus. Dutton/Cobblehill, $15 (0-525-65100-4).

Gr. 5–9. The combination of excitement and straightforward fact makes this book compelling. The text is packed with information on sharks' physical characteristics, behavior, ecology, and survival, while the outstanding photographs offer dramatic views of sharks in the wild.

Coupe, Sheena M. Sharks. 1990. illus. Facts On File, $17.95 (0-8160-2270-4).

Gr. 5–8. Besides the colorful photographs and the well-organized data on the ways of sharks, this large-format book includes information on photographing these often feared fish.

Do Fishes Get Thirsty? Questions Answered by Dr. Les Kaufman and the Staff of the New England Aquarium. 1991. illus. Watts, lib. ed., $14.90 (0-531-10992-5).

Gr. 3–5. Bright white pages make a striking background for the many color photos and diagrams in this selective roundup of aquatic creatures. The text poses and answers an array of often-asked questions: Are there really any sea monsters? Do fishes sleep? and, of course, Do fishes get thirsty?

Ferguson, Ava and **Caillet, Gregor**. Sharks and Rays of the Pacific Coast. 1990. illus. Monterey Bay Aquarium, 886 Cannery Row, Monterey, CA 93940-1085, paper, $8.95 (1-878244-02-7).

Gr. 6–10. Illustrated with excellent color photographs, this well-written book introduces dozens of varieties of sharks and rays found off the coast of Monterey, California.

Gibbons, Gail. Sharks. 1992. illus. Holiday, $14.95 (0-8234-0960-0).

Gr. 1–4. Gibbons offers basic anatomical and life-cycle information as well as specific facts about 12 common shark species. The clear, simple illustrations will appeal to young shark fans.

Guiberson, Brenda Z. Salmon Story. 1993. illus. Holt, $14.95 (0-8050-2754-8).

Gr. 4–7. Guiberson describes the dramatic life cycle of the Pacific salmon, showing how the natural balance worked well for centuries until destroyed by human pollution and interference. The writing is precise and plain, letting the urgent, compelling facts speak for themselves.

Halton, Cheryl M. Those Amazing Eels. 1990. illus. Dillon, lib. ed., $12.95 (0-87518-431-6).

Gr. 4–7. Colorful photos illustrate this well-written introductory book on eels.

Lavies, Bianca. The Atlantic Salmon. 1992. illus. Dutton, $14.50 (0-525-44860-8).

Gr. 2–5. Lavies traces the life cycle of the Atlantic salmon from the fish's beginning as an egg in a stream through its migration to the Atlantic Ocean and its return home to spawn. Dramatic, stage-by-stage photos illustrate the salmon's story.

Maestro, Betsy. Illus. by **Maestro, Giulio**. A Sea Full of Sharks. 1990. Scholastic, $12.95 (0-590-43100-5).

Gr. 2–6 Clear and dramatic, this book combines double-page illustrations in pencil and watercolor with intriguing information on how a great diversity of sharks live, swim, breathe, and feed.

Segaloff, Nat and **Erickson, Paul**. Fish Tales. 1990. Sterling, $12.95 (0-8069-7322-6); lib. ed., $15.69 (0-8069-7323-4).

Gr. 1–3. Illustrated with watercolor paintings, this volume introduces children to the looks, habits, and special adaptations of various fish, from eels to sharks.

Simon, Seymour. Sharks. 1995. illus.

HarperCollins, $15.95 (0-06-023029-0); lib. ed., $15.89 (0-06-023032-0).

Gr. 2–5. With a good balance of text and large full-color photos, Simon introduces the world of sharks. Always informative, he discusses their variety, habits, physical characteristics, and life cycles.

Snedden, Robert. What Is a Fish? 1993. illus. Sierra Club; dist. by Random, $13.95 (0-87156-545-5).

Gr. 2–5. This handsome volume presents fascinating information in large clear type, with bright color photographs and other dramatic illustrations. A series of double-page spreads cover how fish breathe, move, see, and hear underwater; how they reproduce; how and what they eat; and how they keep from being eaten.

Stratton, Barbara R. What Is a Fish? 1991. illus. Watts, $12.95 (0-531-15223-5); lib. ed., $12.90 (0-531-11020-6).

Gr. 3–5. From the New England Aquarium series, this volume provides introductory information about fish, fascinating factoids, and spectacular color photographs. The endpapers pinpoint endangered water habitats on a world map.

Wallace, Karen. Think of an Eel. 1993. illus. Candlewick, $14.95 (1-56402-180-7).

K–Gr.3. Offering information within a fluid narrative, this picture book follows the life cycle of an eel who's born in the Sargasso Sea, migrates to Europe, then returns to its birthplace, where it will mate and then die. Mike Bostock's watercolor paintings illustrate the places and creatures in the text without diminishing the mystery of the eel's journey.

Reptiles

Arnold, Caroline. Illus. by **Hewett, Richard.** Snake. 1991. Morrow, $13.95 (0-688-09409-0); lib. ed., $13.88 (0-688-09410-4).

Gr. 3–6. Setting out the facts while debunking common misconceptions, this clearly written book describes the snake's appearance, structure, life cycle, and behavior. Excellent full-color photographs appear on nearly every page.

Arnosky, Jim. All about Alligators. 1994. illus. Scholastic, $14.95 (0-590-46788-3).

K–Gr.3. Illustrated with watercolor paintings, this book introduces alligators: what they look like, where they live, how they move, and how they help the ecosystem.

Berger, Melvin. Look Out for Turtles! 1992. HarperCollins, $15 (0-06-022539-4); lib. ed., $14.89 (0-06-022540-8).

Gr. 1–4. From the Let's-Read-and-Find-Out Science Book series, this book introduces turtles through an engrossing text and well-labeled color illustrations. Berger includes information about kinds of turtles, their characteristics and life cycles, as well as hints for helping endangered turtles survive.

Clarke, Barry. Amphibian: Eyewitness Books. 1993. illus. Knopf, $16 (0-679-83879-1); lib. ed., $16.99 (0-679-93879-6).

Gr. 4–7. Like other books in the Eyewitness series, this features two-page thematic spreads with many full-color photographs, clear and well captioned, standing out against the bright white pages. Other books in this popular series include *Bird, Elephant, Fish, Mammal, Reptile,* and *Shell.*

Collard, Sneed B. Sea Snakes. 1993. illus. Boyds Mill, $12.95 (1-56397-004-X).

Gr. 4–6. The most common marine reptile is the venomous sea snake, found in the warm waters of the Pacific and Indian Oceans. Illustrated with colorful photos and other illustrations, this book provides a wealth of information about the habits and physiology of the creatures and offers helpful hints on how to behave if you encounter one.

Elliott, Leslee. Really Radical Reptiles & Amphibians. 1995. illus. Sterling, $12.95 (0-8069-1268-5).

Gr. 3–6. Browsers looking for interesting facts and full-color close-ups of familiar and exotic reptiles and amphibians will find this book in the Amazing Animal series very appealing.

Gibbons, Gail. Frogs. 1993. illus. Holiday, $15.95 (0-8234-1052-8); paper, $5.95 (0-8234-1134-6).

K–Gr.3. Bright green borders frame watery scenes where frog spawn changes to embryos, tadpoles, young frogs, and finally, mature amphibians. The clearly written text explains what's happening in Gibbons' distinctive illustrations.

Gibbons, Gail. Sea Turtles. 1995. illus. Holiday, $5.95 (0-8234-1191-5).

K–Gr.4. Gibbons talks about several kinds of sea turtles, how they are alike, and how they differ. Her distinctive watercolor-and-ink illustrations will intrigue young readers.

Gove, Doris. Red-Spotted Newt. 1994. illus. Simon & Schuster/Atheneum, $14.95 (0-689-31697-6).

Gr. 4–8. This well-written narrative reveals the complicated life cycle, habits, and changing physical characteristics of a female red-spotted newt. Detailed watercolor illustrations form the background for the text.

Gove, Doris. A Water Snake's Year. 1991. illus. Simon & Schuster/Atheneum, $13.95 (0-689-31597-X).

Gr. 2–5. Gove describes a year in the life of an adult female snake in Tennessee, detailing month-by-month the activities of this fangless, venomless creature. The elegant language and handsome, naturalistic paintings make this a good choice for reading aloud.

Grace, Eric S. Snakes. 1994. illus. Sierra Club; dist. by Random, $15.95 (0-87156-490-4).

Gr. 4–7. This well-written, oversize book challenges many common misconceptions, clarifies terms such as *cold-blooded*, and explains snake anatomy, classification, hunting, and reproduction, as well as considering the role they play in their ecosystems.

Gravelle, Karen. Lizards. 1991. illus. Watts, lib. ed., $12.90 (0-531-20026-4).

Gr. 3–5. This well-written book describes their widely differing physical features, habitats, food, defenses, and reproduction as well as showing what life is like for many varieties of lizards all over the world.

Lauber, Patricia. Alligators: A Success Story. 1994. illus. Holt, $14.95 (0-8050-1909-X).

Gr. 2–5. With large type, dramatic color photographs, and clear black-and-white drawings, this appealing book introduces the evolution, habitat, physical characteristics, life cycle, and behavior of alligators.

Lavies, Bianca. A Gathering of Garter Snakes. 1993. illus. Dutton, $14.99 (0-525-45099-8).

Gr. 2–6. With superb color photographs and a clear, fact-filled text, Lavies presents snakes in a way that is dramatic without being in any way sensationalist.

Leedy, Loreen. Tracks in the Sand. 1993. illus. Doubleday, $15.95 (0-385-30658-X).

K–Gr.3. Delicately shaded pencil drawings illustrate the story of a sea turtle who crawls onto the shore one night, lays her eggs, and returns to the ocean. The baby turtles hatch out, scramble into the sea, dive, eat, drift, and grow. Years later, one of them crawls onto the same shore one night to lay her eggs. This quiet book not only dramatizes the life cycle of the sea turtle but also respects its dignity.

Maestro, Betsy. Illus. by **Maestro, Jiulio.** Take a Look at Snakes. 1992. Scholastic, $14.95 (0-590-44935-4).

Ages 5–8. The Maestros offer information about the varieties, habitats, behaviors, and physical characteristics of snakes. Watercolor-and-pencil illustrations, appearing on every page, identify individual species and show the traits described in the text.

Markle, Sandra. Inside and Outside Snakes. 1995. illus. Simon & Schuster, $16 (0-02-762315-7).

Gr. 3–6. Markle describes snakes' bodies (inside and out) and behaviors, while the exceptional photos show snakes hiding, hunting, eating, fighting, moving, hatching from their eggs, and shedding their skins.

Martin, James. Chameleons: Dragons in the Trees. 1991. illus. Crown, $13 (0-517-58388-7); lib. ed., $13.99 (0-517-58389-5).

Gr. 2–5. This accessible, large-print book provides intriguing information and remarkable, colorful photographs of chameleons eating, warning, courting, shedding skin, and (of course) camouflaged against bark and foliage.

Maruska, Edward J. Amphibians: Creatures of the Land and Water. 1994. illus. Watts, lib. ed., $14.91 (0-531-11158-X).

Gr. 4–6. Moving beyond the usual pictures of bright-eyed bullfrogs, this book distinguishes itself by treating the three classes of amphibians (salamanders, frogs and toads, and burrowing, wormlike amphibians) separately and in detail.

McClung, Robert M. Snakes: Their Place in the Sun. 1991. illus. Holt, lib. ed., $14.95 (0-8050-1718-6).

Gr. 3–5. A colorful jacket photograph, fairly large print, and many good illustrations give this handbook an inviting look. Though discussion highlights common snakes on a Pennsylvania farm, McClung mentions other species as he explains the life cycle, physical structure, and behavior of snakes.

Parker, Nancy Winslow and **Wright, Joan Richards.** Frogs, Toads, Lizards, and Salamanders. 1990. illus. Greenwillow, $15 (0-688-08680-2); lib. ed., $13.88 (0-688-08681-0).

K–Gr.2. Charming line-and-watercolor artwork illustrates this unusual nature book. Each two-page spread includes a rhyme and picture introducing a young naturalist who finds a reptile or amphibian and a simple, labeled diagram of the animal accompanied by a fact-filled paragraph of basic information.

Parker, Nancy Winslow. Working Frog. 1992. illus. Greenwillow, $15 (0-688-09918-1); lib. ed., $13.93 (0-688-09919-X).

K–Gr.3. "I am a seven-inch, one-pound Bullfrog. I work at the zoo. I would like to tell you about my life." In four colorfully illustrated chapters, Winston describes his capture, his care and feeding at the Bronx Zoo, his waiting days in the holding tank, and his eventual job watching the visitors and sometimes showing off a bit.

Parker, Steve. Frogs and Toads. 1994. illus. Sierra Club; dist. by Little, Brown, $16.95 (0-87156-466-1).

Gr. 3–6. Well designed for browsers, this illustrated book answers common questions about frogs and toads, includes the chapter "25 Essential Facts," and discusses the animals in legends.

Parsons, Alexandra. Amazing Snakes. 1990. illus. Knopf, lib. ed., $9.99 (0-679-90225-2); paper, $7.99 (0-679-80225-8).

Gr. 1–4. Strong on visual content, this book features 10 double-page spreads on individual snakes, with a large, colorful photo of each surrounded by short paragraphs describing it and a few small drawings to show its unusual traits. Other books in the series include *Amazing Lizards, Amazing Spiders, Amazing Birds,* and *Amazing Mammals.*

Patent, Dorothy Hinshaw. Illus. by **Muñoz, William.** The American Alligator. 1994. Clarion, $15.95 (0-395-63392-3).

Gr. 4–6. This handsome book offers an overview of the facts and folklore surrounding alligators and their family, the crocodilians. Complemented by well-chosen full-color photographs on almost every page, the informative text discusses the animal's habits and life cycle.

Pringle, Laurence. Scorpion Man: Exploring the World of Scorpions. 1994. illus. Scribner, $15.95 (0-684-19560-7).

Gr. 4–7. This fascinating book discusses scorpions and profiles biologist Gary Polis, a worldwide authority on these animals. Polis' own vivid, close-up photographs illustrate the book, showing the scorpion in its natural habitat.

Ryder, Joanne. Lizard in the Sun. 1990. illus. Morrow, $13.95 (0-688-07172-4); lib. ed., $13.88 (0-688-07173-2); paper, $4.95 (0-688-13081-X).

K–Gr.2. With precise, poetic language and well-composed illustrations, the picture book tells of a boy who changes into an anole (a chameleonlike lizard) and explores his yard—eating, drinking, running, and hiding.

Simon, Seymour. Snakes. 1992. illus. HarperCollins, $16 (0-06-022529-7); lib. ed., $15.89 (0-06-022530-0); paper, $5.95 (0-06-446165-3).

Gr. 2–5. What does *cold-blooded* mean? How does a snake shed its skin? How does it move and coil? Simon responds to children's fear, fascination, and curiosity about snakes with an informal yet clearly written text. On every other page is a stunning full-color photo, bringing snakes close up for further study.

Snedden, Robert. What Is an Amphibian? 1994. illus. Sierra Club; dist. by Random, $14.95 (0-87156-469-6).

Gr. 3–6. Stunning color photographs and clear diagrams illustrate this introduction to amphibians. The succinct text describes the order's three major families and the special qualities that distinguish them. Another in the series is *What Is a Reptile?*

Winner, Cherie. Salamanders. 1993. illus. Carolrhoda, $19.95 (0-87614-757-0); paper, $6.95 (0-87614-614-0).

Gr. 4–6. Illustrated with color photos, this informative book introduces a variety of salamanders and describes how they live.

Birds

Arnold, Caroline. Illus. by **Hewett, Richard**. Flamingo. 1991. Morrow, $13.95 (0-688-09411-2); lib. ed., $13.88 (0-688-09412-0).

Gr. 3–6. Providing an excellent introduction to the flamingo, this clearly written book includes vivid glimpses of their looks, habits, and special features in the many full-color photographs.

Arnold, Caroline. Illus. by **Hewett, Richard R.** House Sparrows Everywhere. 1992. Carolrhoda, lib. ed., $19.95 (0-87614-696-5).

Gr. 3–6. Exceptionally clear, close-up photos of house sparrows illustrate Arnold's informative discussion of the hidden life of America's most common bird. Also in the series is Arnold's *Ostriches and Other Flightless Birds*.

Arnold, Caroline. On the Brink of Extinction: The California Condor. 1993. illus. Harcourt/Gulliver, lib. ed., $17.95 (0-15-257990-7); paper, $8.95 (0-15-257991-5).

Gr. 3–6. Illustrated with magnificent photos, this lucid history of condors explains the factors that led to the birds' near extinction and the measures taken to reestablish a significant condor breeding population.

Arnosky, Jim. All about Owls. 1995. illus. Scholastic, $14.95 (0-590-46790-5).

K–Gr.3. This colorfully illustrated book describes the owl's physical features and habits as well as providing more information about several American species.

Arnosky, Jim. Crinkleroot's Guide to Knowing the Birds. 1992. illus. Bradbury, $14.95 (0-02-705857-3).

K–Gr.3. Crinkleroot, a lovable woodsman, offers tips on everything from using binoculars to walking quietly through the woods to learning bird anatomy. Arnosky's bright watercolors and precise renderings of different species brighten this attractive book and its companion, *Crinkleroot's 25 Birds Every Child Should Know*.

Bash, Barbara. Urban Roosts. 1990. illus. Sierra Club; dist. by Little, Brown, $15.95 (0-316-08306-2).

Gr. 2–5. This outstanding resource describes and illustrates the ingenious ways that 13 birds find to live in cities. Handsome watercolor paintings feature dramatic perspectives and details of familiar as well as more exotic birds in urban landscapes.

Bernhard, Emery. Eagles: Lions of the Sky. 1994. illus. Holiday, $15.95 (0-8234-1105-2).

Ages 4–8. The eagle is a powerful symbol in many cultures, whether pictured on a postage stamp or on a 1,000-year-old Native American carving. Starting with symbolic images, this dramatic picture book introduces a wealth of factual information about how eagles fly, hunt, migrate, court, mate, nest, and raise their young.

Brown, Fern G. Owls. 1991. illus. Watts, lib. ed., $12.90 (0-531-20008-6).

Gr. 3–6. Illustrated with excellent full-color photos, this book describes the appearance and habits that characterize owls, introducing several species and their distinctive features and behavior.

Brown, Mary Barrett. Wings along the Waterway. 1992. illus. Orchard, $17.95 (0-531-05981-2); lib. ed., $17.99 (0-531-08581-3).

Gr. 3–6. This large-format book highlights 21 water birds, brought to life in Brown's vivid, realistic paintings. Emphasizing the birds' dependence on their particular environments, which range from marshes and wetlands to lagoons, she examines some of the threats to bird survival: predators, diseases, pesticides, pollution, and wetland destruction.

Burton, Jane. See How They Grow: Chick. 1992. illus. Dutton/Lodestar, $6.95 (0-525-67355-5).

Ages 4–8. Written from the chick's point of view ("I am eight days old now. New feathers are growing on my wings"), the text explains the development and learning taking place as the animal grows; meanwhile, the clear color photographs on each bright white page show the dramatic physical changes taking place, step by step. Other books from the See How They Grow series include *Duck*, *Owl*, and *Penguin*.

Capturing Nature. Ed. by Peter Roop and Connie Roop. 1993. illus. Walker, $16.95 (0-8027-8204-3); lib. ed., $17.85 (0-8027-8205-1).

Gr. 5–7. Culled from the diaries of the famous painter and naturalist John James Audubon, this surprisingly lively story tells of Audubon's life as a spoiled child in France, his adventures on the American frontier, his growing fascination with wildlife and art, and his struggles to publish *Birds of America*.

Casey, Denise. Big Birds. 1993. illus. Dutton/Cobblehill, $14.99 (0-525-65121-7).

Gr. 1–3. This book introduces some of the largest birds on earth, including eagles, swans, flamingos, and pelicans. Clear color photographs and generous captions may bring new readers to the text, which presents information in an easy-to-read format. Flowing around the colorful photographs, the text briefly describes the nesting, mating, and eating habits of the birds mentioned.

Demuth, Patricia Brennan. Cradles in the Trees: The Story of Bird Nests. 1994. illus. Macmillan, $14.95 (0-02-728466-2).

Gr. 1–3. Demuth discusses the variety of materials and skills that birds use to create special nests appropriate for sheltering their young. The watercolor-and-pencil artwork illustrates the clearly written text.

Esbensen, Barbara Juster. Great Northern Diver: The Loon. 1990. illus. Little, Brown, $15.95 (0-316-24954-8).

This quiet, elegant picture book introduces the loon. The graceful writing explains this unique bird's appearance and behavior, while the watercolor paintings illustrate the loon's distinctive look and its watery, woodsy habitat.

Esbensen, Barbara Juster. Tiger with Wings: The Great Horned Owl. 1991. illus. Watts/Orchard, $14.95 (0-531-05940-5); lib. ed., $14.99 (0-531-08540-6).

Gr. 2–5. In her graceful, readable text, Esbensen describes the great horned owl's physical characteristics, hunting technique, habits, habitat, and breeding life. Along with the scientific information, she conveys a sense of wonder and respect for the bird. The detailed, realistic watercolors offer handsome portraits of the owl.

Fichter, George S. Cardinals, Robins, and Other Birds. 1994. illus. Golden/Western, $4.95 (0-307-11431-7).

K–Gr.4. This guidebook begins with four illustrated pages discussing bird anatomy from bill to toes, then introduces common North American birds in a series of double-page spreads. A typical entry shows male and female orioles as well as their nest. The relatively large, colorful illustrations make this guide particularly useful for young children.

Fleischman, Paul. Townsend's Warbler. 1992. illus. HarperCollins/Charlotte Zolotow, lib. ed., $12.89 (0-06-021875-4).

Gr. 3–6. Combining American history with natural history, this book describes the 1834 transcontinental journey of two naturalists, John Townsend and Thomas Nuttall. Alternating with the story of hardships and discoveries along their way are accounts of a flock of warblers, migrating from the Pacific Northwest to Mexico and Central America. Attractive maps on the endpapers will help readers follow the naturalists' expedition and the birds' migration.

Ganeri, Anita. Birds. 1992. illus. Watts, lib. ed., $12.60 (0-531-14180-2).

Gr. 3–6. Simple activities combined with a cogent text make this a good resource for children who want to learn about birds. In addition to the precise paintings of birds, diagrams clarify and label the parts of an owl, a wing, and a feather. Other books in the Nature Detective series include Ganeri's *Insects; Plants; Ponds and Pond Life; Small Mammals;* and *Weather.*

Garelick, May. What Makes a Bird a Bird? 1995. illus. Mondo, One Plaza Rd., Greenvale, NY 11548, paper, $4.95 (1-57255-008-2).

Gr. 2–8. Asking strategic questions in a friendly, informal tone, Garelick leads readers to discover what makes a bird a bird. With involving ideas and realistic, close-up illustrations, this book introduces the logic of classification as well as the characteristics of birds.

Gibbons, Gail. The Puffins Are Back! 1991. illus. HarperCollins, $15 (0-06-021603-4); lib. ed., $14.89 (0-06-021604-2).

Gr. 3–4, younger for reading aloud. Gibbons describes the puffin's physical characteristics, behavior, and life cycle.

Colorful pen-and-watercolor paintings show the birds swimming, fishing, and nesting in their Maine environment; scientists are depicted in the course of their research, observing the colony and banding chicks.

Guiberson, Brenda Z. Spotted Owl: Bird of the Ancient Forest. 1994. illus. Holt, $14.95 (0-8050-3171-5).

Gr. 3–6. In discussing the spotted owl, its behavior, and how its survival is threatened, Guiberson also describes the plants and animals of its habitat: the old-growth forests of the Pacific Northwest. A simple yet many-faceted introduction to an endangered species and the complex issues raised by its protection.

Horton, Tom. Swanfall: Journey of the Tundra Swans. 1991. illus. Walker, $15.95 (0-8027-8106-3); lib. ed., $16.85 (0-8027-8107-1).

Gr. 4–6. In addition to telling about tundra swans and their remarkable 1,000-mile migration, the author narrates the life of a swan family for one year. Few nonfiction books offer such graceful prose, vivid descriptions, or clear visual images. Colorful photographs illustrate the text.

If the Owl Calls Again: A Collection of Owl Poems. Ed. by Myra Cohn Livingston. 1990. illus. Macmillan/Margaret K. McElderry, $13.95 (0-689-50501-9).

Gr. 4–7. From reverent Indian chants to jaunty nursery rhymes, from Wordsworth to Prelutsky, this volume celebrates the owl with poetry in many styles and moods.

Jenkins, Priscilla Belz. A Nest Full of Eggs. 1995. illus. HarperCollins, $15 (0-06-023441-5); lib. ed., $14.89 (0-06-023442-3).

Gr. 1–3. In this Let's-Read-and-Find-Out book, two children watch a robin's nest outside the window and read about birds' eggs in their book. The cheerful pencil-and-watercolor illustrations are clear and informative.

Jeunesse, Gallimard and others. Birds. 1993. illus. Scholastic, $10.95 (0-590-46367-5).

Ages 4–8. This small book offers a simple, fact-filled text about birds' beaks, claws, feathers, nests, feeding, and flight. Realistically illustrated with sharp, colorful pictures on strong white paper, the spiral-bound pages make ingenious use of brightly painted transparencies that reveal surprising changes and connections as you turn the pages.

Lang, Aubrey. Eagles. 1990. illus. Sierra Club; dist. by Little, Brown, $14.95 (0-316-51387-3).

Gr. 4–6. Attractive and useful, this oversize book includes range maps and diagrams, outstanding color photographs, and a well-organized text discussing the eagle's physical appearance, behavior patterns, reproductive habits, and likely future.

Lavies, Bianca. Tundra Swans. 1994. illus. Dutton, $15.99 (0-525-45273-7).

Gr. 4–6. The book describes the swans themselves as well as the efforts of a scientific team to band the birds and track their migratory route from Chesapeake Bay to the Arctic tundra. Beautifully lit photographs show swans in the air and on the water.

Lerner, Carol. Backyard Birds of Winter. 1994. illus. Morrow, $16 (0-688-12819-X); lib. ed., $15.93 (0-688-12820-3).

Gr. 3–5. This handsome introduction to birds in winter begins with a discussion of how their anatomy and behavior help them survive the cold weather in northern climates, while the heart of the book presents the physical features, diets, habits, and ranges of more than two dozen relatively common species.

Precise watercolor paintings of birds make this a beautiful as well as a practical way to learn about wildlife that even city children can observe.

McMillan, Bruce. A Beach for the Birds. 1993. illus. Houghton, lib. ed., $15.95 (0-395-64050-4).

Gr. 3–6. McMillan describes the least tern, a species of endangered sea swallows that summer along the North Atlantic coast: their life cycle, habitat, food requirements, predators, and behaviors. Superb photographs include amazing shots of birds diving for prey and creating scrapes in the sand for soon-to-be-laid eggs, as well as close-ups of young hatchlings.

McMillan, Bruce. Nights of the Pufflings. 1995. illus. Houghton, $14.95 (0-395-70810-9).

Gr. 2–4. McMillan takes readers to an island off the coast of Iceland where every year, on nights when the youngest puffins (called pufflings) take their first flights, the children organize to rescue birds who don't make it to the sea. The crisp clarity, the quality of light, and the beautiful landscapes make every photo a special one.

McMillan, Bruce. Penguins at Home: Gentoos of Antarctica. 1993. illus. Houghton, $15.95 (0-395-66560-4).

Gr. 3–6. In this effective photo-essay, McMillan presents the Gentoo penguins in their Antarctic habitat. The full-color photographs work closely with the text to illustrate aspects of Gentoo physiology and behavior.

Patent, Dorothy Hinshaw. Illus. by **Muñoz, William**. Feathers. 1992. Dutton/Cobblehill, $15 (0-525-65081-4).

This appealing book, with its briskly moving text and exceptionally clear photos, presents feathers: their characteristics, their use in flight and camouflage, and their role in human history.

Patent, Dorothy Hinshaw. Looking at Penguins. 1993. illus. Holiday, $15.95 (0-8234-1037-4).

Gr. 3–5. Good, clear photographs illustrate this introduction to penguins, which discusses basic facts about the birds, introduces several different kinds, and considers threats to their survival. The photos clearly show the penguins' surroundings and capture differences among species.

Patent, Dorothy Hinshaw. Illus. by **Muñoz, William**. Ospreys. 1993. Clarion, $14.95 (0-395-63391-5).

Gr. 4–7. Patent discusses the physical characteristics, general behavior, and life cycle of these birds of prey, paying particular attention to their feeding (spectacular dives for fish) and nesting habits (their huge nests can weigh up to half a ton). Muñoz's distinctive color photographs complement the text.

Patent, Dorothy Hinshaw. Illus. by **Muñoz, William**. Pelicans. 1992. Clarion, $14.95 (0-395-57224-X).

Gr. 4–6. "A pelican is flight transformed," begins Patent's natural-history book, which boasts excellent full-color photos and concise descriptions of pelican characteristics, types, and behaviors.

Peters, Lisa Westberg. This Way Home. 1994. illus. Holt, $14.95 (0-8050-1368-7).

Ages 5–8. Lovely watercolors illustrate a simple, lyrical text that chronicles the first migratory flight of a flock of young sparrows. Using the sun, the stars, and the earth's magnetic field as compasses, the feathered navigators travel more than a thousand miles from the prairie grasslands of Minnesota to the Gulf Coast.

Sattler, Helen Roney. The Book of North American Owls. 1995. illus. Clarion, $15.95 (0-395-60524-5).

Gr. 3–6. Amply illustrated with colored-pencil and watercolor artwork, this large-format book introduces the physical features and habits of North American owls. This attractive book is intriguing to read and well designed for research.

Selsam, Millicent E. and **Hunt, Joyce**. A First Look at Ducks, Geese, and Swans. 1990. illus. Walker, $11.95 (0-8027-6975-6); lib. ed., $12.85 (0-8027-6976-4).

Gr. 1–3. In this series, which includes *A First Look at Bats*, the authors aim to show children the search for differences that is the basis for scientific classification. Here they focus on features shared by ducks, geese, and swans (webbed feet, etc.) and on how these species can be differentiated by their size, form, and markings. Softly shaded pencil drawings illustrate the text and form the basis for comparison.

Snedden, Robert. What Is a Bird? 1993. illus. Sierra Club; dist. by Little, Brown, $13.95 (0-87156-539-0).

Gr. 3–5. Striking color photographs, a crisp layout, and a straightforward, lucid text combine to provide a direct answer to the title question, What is a bird? "They all have beaks. They all have wings. . . . The females all lay eggs. . . . They all have feathers." In addition to the basic definition, Snedden provides details about each of these characteristics and provides an accurate, easy-to-understand explanation of flight.

Taylor, Barbara. The Bird Atlas. 1993. illus. Dorling Kindersley, $19.95 (1-56458-327-9).

Gr. 4–9. This oversize, continent-by-continent pictorial guide to the world's birds presents colorful maps highlighted with illustrations of particular species. The brief text describes the birds' characteristics and behavior. At the end of the book are sections on migratory flight and endangered birds.

Mammals

Arnold, Caroline. Illus. by **Hewett, Richard.** Monkey. 1993. Morrow, $15 (0-688-11342-7); lib. ed., $14.93 (0-688-11343-5).

Gr. 3–6. The clear, succinct text describes a monkey's physical characteristics, natural habitats, reproductive cycles, communication, relationship to other, similar species, and the outlook for continued survival in the wild. The striking color photos capture an array of expressions and behaviors. Arnold and Hewett's excellent animal series also includes *Camel, Elephant, Orangutan,* and *Panda.*

Arnold, Caroline. Illus. by **Hewett, Richard.** Sea Lion. 1994. Morrow, $15 (0-688-12027-X); lib. ed., $14.93 (0-688-12028-8).

Gr. 3–5. This book begins with two sea lions brought to a marine mammal rescue center and ends with their release, but in between it broadens out to consider other sea lions, their characteristics, habits, food, and natural enemies. *Killer Whale, Lion,* and *Rhino* are other books by Arnold and Hewett in this series, which features clear, full-color photography and lucid, well-organized writing.

Arnosky, Jim. Crinkleroot's 25 Mammals Every Child Should Know. 1994. illus. Bradbury, $12.95 (0-02-705845-X).

Gr. 1–4. In this cheerful picture book, rumpled woodsman Crinkleroot introduces children to mammals, from human to elephant to whale. The lively watercolor artwork is precise yet informal, as is the writing.

Arnosky, Jim. Long Spikes. 1992. illus. Clarion, $12.70 (0-395-58830-8).

Gr. 4–7. After their mother's death, yearling buck Long Spikes and his sister travel together as spring melts into summer. She leaves to join a group of does. As autumn advances, Long Spikes searches for a mate, witnesses the sparring of other bucks, escapes the bullets of hunters, and narrowly defeats a group of hungry coyotes. This story takes readers into the forest to experience it as a deer might.

Bare, Colleen Stanley. Elephants on the Beach. 1990. illus. Dutton/Cobblehill, $12.95 (0-525-65018-0).

K–Gr.3. Crisp color photos and clearly written text distinguish this elementary introduction to the elephant seal.

Bare, Colleen Stanley. Never Grab a Deer by the Ear. 1993. illus. Dutton/Cobblehill, $13 (0-525-65112-8).

Gr. 1–4. Neatly framed color photos illustrate this introductory book on deer. The smoothly flowing narrative includes the species and geographical locations of the deer family, physical characteristics, behavior, and the differences between antlers and horns.

Berman, Ruth. American Bison. 1992. illus. Carolrhoda, lib. ed., $19.95 (0-87614-697-3).

Gr.3–5. This informative book tells of the near extinction and conservation of the bison as well as the natural history of the animal. Young readers will appreciate the colorful, close-up photographs and large type in the Nature Watch series, which includes Stuart's *Bats* and *The Astonishing Armadillo.*

Bernhard, Emery. Reindeer. 1994. illus. Holiday, $15.95 (0-8234-1097-8).

Gr. 1–4. Large typeface, generous design, and watercolor illustrations enhance this clear, absorbing discussion of the life cycle of the reindeer including information about the animal's habits and habitat.

Bonners, Susan. Hunter in the Snow: The Lynx. 1994. illus. Little, Brown, $14.95 (0-316-10201-6).

Gr. 2–4. This unsentimental picture book follows a single female lynx through one year of her life: hunting, mating, giving birth, caring for her young, and teaching them the skills they will need to survive. Soft-edged yet realistic pastel drawings give visual appeal to the informative story.

Brandenburg, Jim. To the Top of the World: Adventures with Arctic Wolves. 1993. illus. Walker, $16.95 (0-8027-8219-1); lib. ed., $17.85 (0-8027-8220-5).

Gr. 5–7. This compelling photo-essay chronicles a wildlife photographer's experience living close to an Arctic wolf pack. Intimate, full-color photos show pups playing, adults engorging themselves on a fresh kill, and the pack having a howling songfest. Brandenburg's respect and awe are apparent in every vivid paragraph and picture.

Bunting, Eve. Illus. by **Minor, Wendell**. Red Fox Running. 1993. Houghton, $15.95 (0-395-58919-3).

Ages 4–8. Bunting's verse tells of a hungry fox who hunts through a winter's day and night until he kills a bobcat to bring home to his family. As naturalistic and delicate as the text, Minor's full-color artwork captures with precision the sights of the rural landscape.

Clark, Margaret Goff. The Endangered Florida Panther. 1993. illus. Dutton/Cobblehill, $14.99 (0-525-65114-4).

Gr. 4–8. Many color photos illustrate this introduction to the endangered and reclusive Florida panther. Clark explains how wildlife biologists study the breed in its natural environment and remove some of the young for selective breeding in captivity.

Clark, Margaret Goff. The Vanishing Manatee. 1990. illus. Dutton/Cobblehill, $14 (0-525-65024-5).

Gr. 4–7. Illustrated with many photos, this book balances description of the manatee's physiology with discussion of threats to the animal's survival and attempts to protect it.

Cossi, Olga. Harp Seals. 1991. illus. Carolrhoda, lib. ed., $19.95 (0-87614-437-7); paper, $6.95 (0-87614-567-5).

Gr. 3–6. Written with clarity and illustrated with full-color photographs, this book describes the life cycle, migratory patterns, and behavior of the North Atlantic harp seal.

Darling, Kathy. Manatee. 1991. Lothrop, $14.95 (0-688-09030-3); lib. ed., $14.88 (0-688-09031-1).

Gr. 3–7. Full-color underwater photographs illustrate this discussion of the manatee's life cycle, behavior, and physical characteristics, as well as the threats to its survival.

Darling, Kathy. Tasmanian Devil: On Location. 1992. illus. Lothrop, $15 (0-688-09726-X); lib. ed., $14.93 (0-688-09727-8).

Gr. 3–5. This excellent book discusses the Tasmanian devil: its life cycle, behavior patterns, eating habits, range, and outlook for long-term survival. Superb full-color photographs (many taken at night) on nearly every page portray these creatures engaging in a variety of activities. Other books in the series include Darling's *Kangaroos* and *Walrus: On Location*.

DaVolls, Linda. Tano & Binti: Two Chimpanzees Return to the Wild. 1994. illus. Clarion, $14.95 (0-395-68701-2).

K–Gr.3. Illustrated with pastels, this

eloquent story (based on a real incident) tells of two young chimpanzees born in the London Zoo and returned to a forest in Central Africa. The young brother and sister are bewildered when they first arrive in their new home, but an adult chimp nurtures them and shows them how to survive in the wild.

Dolphins. Ed. by Cousteau Society staff. 1992. illus. Simon & Schuster, $3.95 (0-671-77062-4).

K–Gr.3. This appealing little book offers full-color photographs and minimal text introducing the bottlenose dolphin, its physical features and behavior.

Dorros, Arthur. Elephant Families. 1994. illus. HarperCollins, $15 (0-06-022948-9); lib. ed., $14.89 (0-06-022949-7); paper, $4.95 (0-06-445122-4).

Gr. 2–3. From the Let's-Read-and-Find-Out series, this compact book introduces African elephants, emphasizing their family structure and individual and group behavior, including how they care for their young. Full-color, line-and-wash illustrations effectively illustrate the text.

Douglas-Hamilton, Oria. The Elephant Family Book. 1990. illus. Picture Book Studio, $15.95 (0-88708-126-6).

Gr. 3–5. Many beautiful photographs illustrate this informative book, which introduces a family of elephants living in Tanzania's Lake Manyara National Park, follows them on their round of activities, discusses the animals' physiology and fascinating social structure, and communicates the author's concern for this endangered species. Other books in the series include Hoshino's *The Grizzly Bear Family Book* and Scott's *The Leopard Family Book*.

Dow, Lesley. Whales. 1990. illus. Facts On File, $17.95 (0-8160-2271-2).

Gr. 5–8. This oversize volume, filled with color photos and well-organized information, includes discussions of legends and of familial relationships. Lumpkin's *Small Cats* is another book in the excellent Great Creatures of the World series.

Earle, Ann. Zipping, Zapping, Zooming Bats. 1995. illus. HarperCollins, $15 (0-06-023479-2); lib. ed., $14.89 (0-06-023480-6).

K–Gr.2. Colorful artwork illustrates this succinct introduction to the little brown bat, the most common in the U.S. After discussing their wing structure, claws, echolocation, grooming, diet, hibernation, nursing, loss of habitat, and endangerment, Earle supplies simple plans for building a bat house.

Esbensen, Barbara Juster. Baby Whales Drink Milk. 1994. illus. HarperCollins, $15 (0-06-021551-8); lib. ed., $14.99 (0-06-021552-6); paper, $4.95 (0-06-445119-4).

K–Gr.2. Simple and informative, this book tells how whales are like other mammals and unlike fish, then briefly introduces a full range of information about whale anatomy, development, and behavior. Colorful paintings show the animals in their habitat, a whale model in a museum, and a map of migration.

Esbensen, Barbara Juster. Playful Slider. 1993. illus. Little, Brown, $15.95 (0-316-24977-7).

Gr. 1–3. Following the travels of two otters in the wild, this informative book describes the life of the North American river otter as the seasons change—its home, feeding habits, and reproductive cycle. Colorful artwork illustrates this handsome book.

Gallardo, Evelyn. Among the Orangutans: The Birutée Galdikas Story. 1993. illus. Chronicle/Byron, lib. ed., $12.95 (0-8118-0031-8); paper, $6.95 (0-8118-0408-9).

Gr. 4–7. The third of the triumvirate

known as Leakey's Primates (Dian Fossey and Jane Goodall were the other two), Galdikas chose as her subject the elusive orangutan, which she began studying in 1971. This book offers an admiring picture of Galdikas' world, illustrated with sharp, often fascinating photos.

George, Jean Craighead. Animals Who Have Won Our Hearts. 1994. illus. HarperCollins, $15 (0-06-021543-7); lib. ed., $14.89 (0-06-021544-5).

Gr. 3–6. George recounts the stories of 10 famous or beloved animals, including Koko, a gorilla that learned sign language. In short chapters, she describes each animal and its unusual good deed or act of bravery. Each section includes one color portrait and several smaller black-and-white drawings.

George, Jean Craighead. The Moon of the Mountain Lions. Rev. ed. 1991. HarperCollins, $14.95 (0-06-022429-0); lib. ed., $14.89 (0-06-022438-X).

Gr. 3–6. A handsome book with 10 full-page paintings, this revitalization of the Thirteen Moons series includes a rewritten text and new full-color illustrations. Here George follows the path of the mountain lion through 28 days, creating a story that incorporates information about its habits and habitat. Each of the 12 other books in the series focuses on another animal, including the alligator, the gray wolf, and the winter bird.

Gibbons, Gail. Whales. 1991. illus. Holiday, $15.95 (0-8234-0900-7); paper, $5.95 (0-8234-1030-7).

K–Gr.2. Clear, captioned paintings illustrate Gibbons' straightforward discussion of whales: what they look like, where they live, how they move, what they sound like, and why they have been hunted by humans.

Gibbons, Gail. Wolves. 1994. illus. Holiday, $15.95 (0-8234-1127-3).

Gr. 2–4. Using her effective format of large color drawings and a text packed with nuggets of information, Gibbons explores the life of the gray wolf (or timber wolf). She discusses its habitat (which has been greatly decreased over the last several centuries), appearance, hunting, diet, communication systems, social order, reproduction, and relationships with humans.

Gilks, Helen. Bears. 1993. illus. Ticknor & Fields, $15.95 (0-395-66899-9).

Gr. 2–5. This oversize book introduces eight types of bears, showing how they look in beautifully detailed illustrations and discussing their characteristics and behavior in clearly written text and captions. Another in the series is Lemmon's *Apes.*

Hall, Katy and **Eisenberg, Lisa.** Illus. by **Rubel, Nicole.** Batty Riddles. 1993. Dial, $11.99 (0-8037-1217-0); lib. ed., $11.89 (0-8037-1218-9).

Gr. 2–4. Illustrated wtih wonderfully bizarre artwork, this collection of riddles about bats includes a lively mix of the clever, the dumb, and the in-between.

Halton, Cheryl M. Those Amazing Bats. 1991. illus. Dillon, lib. ed., $12.95 (0-87518-458-8).

Gr. 3–6. Clear writing and excellent color photos make this an excellent introduction to the ways of bats and the study of bats.

Hiller, Ilo. Introducing Mammals to Young Naturalists. 1990. illus. Texas A & M Univ., $9 (0-89096-427-0); paper, $4.50 (0-89096-428-9).

Gr. 5–9. This attractive book of illustrated articles, most written for *Texas Parks and Wildlife* magazine, introduces readers to a variety of mammals. Some, like javelinas and armadillos, are regional creatures, while skunks, squirrels, and red foxes have a much broader range. The last chapter suggests word games and art projects.

Hoyt, Erich. Illus. by **Folkens, Pieter.** Meeting the Whales: The Equinox Guide to Giants of the Deep. 1991. Camden; dist. by Firefly, $17.95 (0-921820-23-2); paper, $9.95 (0-921820-23-2).

Gr. 5–10. Attractive enough for browsing and informative enough for research, this guide to whales offers exceptionally clear full-color photographs and paintings, good explanatory captions, and a well-organized text.

If You Ever Meet a Whale. Illus. by **Fisher, Leonard Everett** Ed. by Myra Cohn Livingston. 1992. illus. Holiday, $14.95 (0-8234-0940-6).

Gr. 1–3. Though this handsome book offers 17 poems from many sources, including the traditional ballads of the Greenland Eskimos and the Nootka Indians, most of the poems were written by modern American poets. Fisher's majestic full-color paintings depict the underwater world in deep, cool hues.

Jauck, Andrea and **Points, Larry.** Assateague: Island of the Wild Ponies. 1993. illus. Macmillan, $14.95 (0-02-774695-X).

Gr. 2–4. Beginning with the birth of new foals in the spring, this photo-essay follows events in a year in the life of wild horses. The connection with Marguerite Henry's *Misty of Chincoteague* novels will make this a good choice for her readers.

Knight, Lindsay. The Sierra Club Book of Great Mammals. 1992. illus. Sierra Club; dist. by Random, lib. ed., $16.95 (0-87156-507-2).

Gr. 3–6. This large-size volume of photo-essays has the bright appearance of a magazine, with dramatic color photographs and an informal, enthusiastic text that relays a great deal of factual information.

Kraus, Scott and **Mallory, Kenneth.** The Search for the Right Whale. 1993. illus. Crown, $14 (0-517-57844-1); lib. ed., $14.99 (0-517-57845-X).

Gr. 3–6. The authors, a scientist and a science writer from the New England Aquarium, take readers aboard their research boat to observe the North Atlantic right whales and to learn what biologists have discovered about them and their migration. Clear color photographs and maps illustrate this intriguing book.

Lauber, Patricia. Great Whales: The Gentle Giants. 1991. illus. Holt, lib. ed., $14.95 (0-8050-1717-8).

Gr. 3–5. Printed in fairly large type and illustrated with drawings and photos (many in color), this appealing handbook explains the characteristics and habits of great whales and discusses the history of whale hunting and conservation efforts.

Lawrence, R. D. Wolves. 1990. illus. Sierra Club; dist. by Little, Brown, $16.95 (0-316-51676-7); paper, $7.95 (0-316-51677-5).

Gr. 4–6. A slim, oversize volume, this tells about the appearance, behavior, habits, and likely future of wolves. Outstanding color photographs, supported by range maps and diagrams, will capture interest.

Lepthien, Emilie U. Woodchucks. 1992. illus. Childrens Press, lib. ed., $12.95 (0-516-01140-5); paper, $4.95 (0-516-41191-8).

Gr. 2–3. Large print and colorful photos will please young readers of this introductory book on the woodchuck, or groundhog. Other animal books in the New True series include Lepthien's *Squirrels* and *Opossums.*

Lewin, Ted. Tiger Trek. 1990. illus. Macmillan, $14.95 (0-02-757381-8).

K–Gr.4. Through brief text and intriguing watercolor paintings, this book takes readers along the path of a tiger as she stalks her prey in the wilds of India.

Lindblad, Lisa. The Serengeti Migration: Africa's Animals on the Move. 1994. Hyperion; dist. by Little, Brown, $15.95 (1-56282-668-9); lib. ed., $15.89 (1-562882-669-7).

Gr. 3–7. Readers can almost feel the earth trembling beneath the thundering hooves of wildebeest and zebra as the animals migrate through Tanzania and Kenya. Spectacular photos illustrate the brief, incisive text in this impressive book.

Lucas, Eileen. Jane Goodall: Friend of the Chimps. 1992. illus. Millbrook, $11.90 (1-56294-135-6).

Gr. 3–5. Attractively illustrated with many photographs, this attractive biography not only profiles Goodall but also describes how chimps behave in the wild and how she got close enough to study them.

Maynard, Thane. Primates: Apes, Monkeys, Prosimians. 1995. illus. Watts, lib. ed., $14.95 (0-531-11169-5).

Gr. 4–6. Profusely illustrated with large, beautiful photographs, this book presents individual species of primates, focusing on their distinguishing characteristics, social behavior, and preferred environment.

McMillan, Bruce. Going on a Whale Watch. 1992. illus. Scholastic, lib. ed., $14.95 (0-590-45768-3).

K–Gr.3. This book takes readers out to sea on a whale-watch boat. While clear full-color photographs document whale anatomy and behavior as seen above the water's surface, smaller diagrams show what is happening underwater at the same time.

Milton, Joyce. Big Cats. 1994. illus. Putnam/Grosset, $7.99 (0-448-40565-2);

paper, $3.50 (0-448-40564-4).

Gr. 1–3. This book features dramatic full-color illustrations and a simple text discussing leopards, tigers, lions, jaguars, cougars, and cheetahs. Another in the All Aboard Reading series is Demuth's Snakes.

Parker, Steve. Whales and Dolphins. 1994. illus. Sierra Club; dist. by Little, Brown, $16.95 (0-87156-465-3).

Gr. 3–6. Chock-full of information as well as colorful paintings, photos, and diagrams, this large-format book uses fold-out pages to illustrate whales.

Parsons, Alexandra. Illus. by **Young, Jerry.** Amazing Mammals. 1990. Knopf, lib. ed., $7.99 (0-679-90224-4).

Gr. 1–4. The appealing layout of this introductory book on mammals consists of thematic double-page spreads with a large photo of an animal surrounded by smaller photos and drawings captioned by short paragraphs of text. Other books in the series include Parsons' Amazing Birds and Amazing Spiders.

Patent, Dorothy Hinshaw. African Elephants: Giants of the Land. 1991. Holiday, $14.95 (0-8234-0911-2).

Gr. 2–5. Illustrated with colorful photos, this well-researched book discusses elephants, their life in the wild, and the question of their survival.

Patent, Dorothy Hinshaw. Illus. by **Muñoz, William.** Deer and Elk. 1994. Clarion, $15.95 (0-395-52003-7).

Gr. 3–6. After defining common characteristics of the deer family, Patent devotes chapters to white-tailed deer, mule deer, and elk as well as to preservation issues. Photographs offer striking glimpses of the animals in their natural habitat.

Patent, Dorothy Hinshaw. Illus. by **Muñoz, William.** Gray Wolf, Red Wolf. 1990. Clarion, $15.95 (0-89919-863-5);

paper, $6.95 (0-395-69627-5).

Gr. 4–7. Illustrated with clear, full-color photos, this attractive study covers North America's two native species of wolf, the gray and the red. Patent discusses their physical characteristics, social structure, uneasy relationship with human beings, and current endangered status.

Patent, Dorothy Hinshaw. Killer Whales. 1993. illus. Holiday, $15.95 (0-8234-0999-6).

Gr. 2–4. Capturing the grace of a killer whale breaching or the beauty of a tranquil pod resting in British Columbian waters, this book's excellent photos extend the lucid text, which discusses the orcas' physiology, sonar communication, and family units.

Patent, Dorothy Hinshaw. Illus. by **Muñoz, William.** Looking at Bears. 1994. Holiday, $15.95 (0-8234-1139-7).

Gr. 2–5. With clear, direct prose and action color photographs on almost every page, this book discusses bear evolution, endangerment, classification, habitat, and behavior, particularly hibernation, reproduction, and nutrition.

Patent, Dorothy Hinshaw. Illus. by **Muñoz, William.** Prairie Dogs. 1993. Clarion, $15.45 (0-395-56572-3).

Gr. 3–6. In this effective book, Patent describes the varieties, features, habits, habitats, and predators of prairie dogs, while the full-color photographs take readers out to the prairie for clear views of its plants and animals.

Patent, Dorothy Hinshaw. Seals, Sea Lions and Walruses. 1990. illus. Holiday, $14.95 (0-8234-0834-5).

Gr. 4–6. Illustrated with many black-and-white photos, this book clearly explains the similarities and differences between the three species of pinnipeds and discusses each one in terms of its habitat, appearance, physiology, food, mating, and care of young.

Patent, Dorothy Hinshaw. Illus. by **Muñoz, William.** Why Mammals Have Fur. 1995. Dutton/Cobblehill, $14.99 (0-525-65141-1).

Gr. 3–5. The brief, well-focused text discusses the many forms of fur and their contributions to the success of mammals, whether for warmth, camouflage, or weaponry (e.g., the rhinoceros horn and the porcupine quill). Simple and clear, the full-color photographs extend the text and add greatly to the book's appeal.

Payne, Katharine. Elephants Calling. 1992. illus. Crown, $14 (0-517-58175-2); lib. ed., $14.99 (0-517-58176-0).

Gr. 3–5. This slender volume offers intriguing glimpses of a scientist at work. Payne, who discovered that elephants were making sounds below the register of human hearing, discusses the behavior of elephants in the wild. The excellent photographs focus mainly on a particular baby elephant and his extended family, showing how they act and interact.

Pringle, Laurence. Illus. by **Tuttle, Merlin D.** Batman: Exploring the World of Bats. 1991. Scribner, $14.95 (0-684-19232-2).

Gr. 3–6. Combining biography and lively science writing, Pringle profiles bat expert Merlin Tuttle. Extraordinary full-color photos illustrate the book, which highlights the scientist's experiences studying bats and gives intriguing information about bat behavior as well as a sense of the destructive forces bats face in the modern world.

Pringle, Laurence. Jackal Woman: Exploring the World of Jackals. 1993. Scribner, $14.95 (0-684-19435-X).

Gr. 5–7. Pringle describes the work of Patricia Moehlman, a zoologist researching the jackal. Beautiful color photographs illustrate this account, which expresses the scientist's excitement about her work and the admiration she feels for her subjects as well as providing information about the habits and characteristics of jackals.

Rounds, Glen. Wild Horses. 1993. illus. Holiday, $14.95 (0-8234-1019-6).

K–Gr.3. With his well-known angular lines, weathered colors, and sparse detail, Rounds presents a stirring season-to-season account of a beautiful vanishing animal.

Ryden, Hope. Your Cat's Wild Cousins. 1992. illus. Dutton/Lodestar, $16 (0-525-67354-7).

Gr. 3–5. Photographer and naturalist Ryden explains some of the similarities and differences between a domestic cat and its wild relatives, following up with a closer look at 18 different feline species.

Ryder, Joanne. Sea Elf. 1993. Morrow, $15 (0-688-10060-0); lib. ed., $14.93 (0-688-10061-9).

K–Gr.3. From Ryder's Just for a Day series, this picture book asks readers to imagine being transformed into a sea otter. The poetic text is well supported by vivid paintings of the California cove the otter calls home.

Ryder, Joanne. Winter Whale. 1991. Morrow, $13.95 (0-688-07176-7); lib. ed., $13.88 (0-688-07177-5).

K–Gr.3. Running along the seashore in Hawaii, a young boy is transformed into a humpback whale. In clear, poetic language, Ryder describes the graceful creature's movement through the sea and his haunting song. Expressive acrylic paintings bring the fantasy to life.

Sattler, Helen Roney. Giraffes, the Sentinels of the Savannas. 1990. illus. Lothrop, $14.95 (0-688-08284-X); lib. ed., $14.88 (0-688-08285-8).

Gr. 3–7. Sattler draws on her skills as a keen observer and a fine writer in this intriguing introduction to the giraffe. Graceful and accurate sepia-tone illustrations add to the beauty of the book.

Schlaepfer, Gloria G and **Samuelson, Mary Lou**. African Rhinos. 1992. illus. Dillon, lib. ed., $12.95 (0-87518-505-3).

Gr. 3–5. Illustrated with colorful, vivid photographs, this book offers plenty of information about the rhino's evolution, adaptation, habitat, and behavior, as well as the danger of extinction. Other books in the Remarkable Animals series include Pembleton's The Armadillo and Sherrow's The Porcupine.

Schneider, Jost. Lynx. 1994. illus. Carolrhoda, lib. ed., $14.96 (0-87614-844-5).

Gr. 4–7. Schneider's extraordinary photographs will appeal to cat lovers as well as to readers seeking information on the lynx and other predators. In eight chapters, the author covers topics such as population, hunting, and raising young.

Schoenherr, John. Bear. 1991. illus. Putnam/Philomel, $14.95 (0-399-22177-8).

K–Gr.3. Delicately lined watercolors enhance this quiet story of a young bear in the Alaskan wilderness. Separated from his mother and attacked by several animals, the cub survives and learns to catch salmon on his own.

Schomp, Virginia. The Bottlenose Dolphin. 1994. illus. Silver Burdett, lib. ed., $13.95 (0-87518-605-X).

Gr. 3–5. This book conveys the grace and intelligence of the bottlenose dolphin through captioned color photos and a very readable text.

Seals. Ed. by Cousteau Society staff. 1992. illus. Simon & Schuster, $3.95 (0-671-77061-6).

K–Gr.3. An appealing introduction, this little book features colorful photographs and minimal text describing the characteristics and behavior of seals.

Sherrow, Victoria. Endangered Mammals of North America. 1995. illus. Twenty-First Century, lib. ed., $18.98 (0-8050-3253-3).

Gr. 5–8. Sherrow begins by discussing mammals, the worldwide problem of lost habitats and pollution, and the controversy surrounding the Endangered Species Act. In the chapters that follow, she focuses on one species, such as Caribbean manatees, bowhead whales, gray wolves, black-tailed prairie dogs, and Florida panthers. Colorful photographs and habitat maps appear throughout the book.

Sibbald, Jean H. The Manatee. 1990. illus. Dillon, lib. ed., $13.95 (0-87518-429-4).

Gr. 4–7. Illustrated with full-color pictures, this book introduces the manatee, giving information about the appearance and behavior of the animal as well as a you-are-there profile of a particular West Indian manatee.

The Sierra Club Book of Small Mammals. Ed. by Lindsay Knight. 1993. illus. Sierra Club; dist. by Random, $16.95 (0-87156-525-0).

Gr. 5–7. This oversize book organizes small mammals within broader groups, such as insect-eaters, canids, and rodents, and discusses each animal in a few concise paragraphs that describe its size, habits, and geographical range. Most are pictured in a colorful photo or a detailed drawing.

Simon, Seymour. Big Cats. 1991. illus. HarperCollins, $17 (0-06-021646-8); lib. ed., $16.89 (0-06-021647-6); paper, $5.95 (0-06-446119-X).

K–Gr.3. Simon introduces seven large cats, noting their similarities and differences. Illustrating the clearly written text are stunning color photos of the lion, tiger, leopard, jaguar, puma, cheetah, and snow leopard.

Simon, Seymour. Wolves. 1993. illus. HarperCollins, $16 (0-06-022531-9); lib. ed., $15.89 (0-06-022534-3).

Gr. 2-4. This photo-essay includes dramatic action pictures, splendidly reproduced in full color, facing pages of text that give basic information on topics such as how wolves live in the natural world, what they look like, how they hunt, and how they rear their young.

Snedden, Robert. What Is a Mammal? 1994. illus. Sierra Club; dist. by Random, $14.95 (0-87156-468-8).

Gr. 3–6. Illustrated with stunning color photos in an appealing format, this book discusses the characteristics of mammals.

Wallace, Karen. Think of a Beaver. 1993. illus. Candlewick, $14.95 (1-56402-179-3).

K–Gr.2. This picture book shows how North American beavers swim, build dams, signal one another, raise their young, and live through the winter. The activities shown in Mick Manning's expressive line-and-watercolor illustrations will intrigue young children.

Waters, John F. Watching Whales. 1991. illus. Dutton/Cobblehill, $14.95 (0-525-65072-5).

Gr. 3–5. Waters discusses the development of whale-watching on the eastern coast of the U.S., relates a story about a school class that adopts a whale and goes whale-watching, and describes the winter of 1987–88, when 15 humpback whales died in the Atlantic. Full-color photographs appear on nearly every page.

Author Index

Author Index

Stangl, Jean, 21.
Stannard, Russell, 10.
Staub, Frank, 32.
Stock, Catherine, 52.
Stratton, Barbara R., 54.
Stwertka, Albert, 15.
Swanson, Diane, 32.
Swedberg, Jack, 44.
Taylor, Barbara, 32, 47, 63.
Taylor, Dave, 47.
Tesar, Jenny, 32.
Tresselt, Alvin, 37.
Tuttle, Merlin D., 70.
Twist, Clint, 32.
Van Rose, Susanna, 21.
VanCleave, Janice, 15, 21, 25, 33.

Vare, Ethlie Ann, 15.
Vecchione, Glen, 16.
Vieira, Linda, 37.
Voake, Charlotte, 50.
Vogel, Carole Garbuny, 33.
Vogt, Gregory L., 11.
Wadsworth, Ginger, 33.
Walker, Sally M., 21.
Wallace, Karen, 54, 72.
Waters, John F., 21, 72.
Watts, Barrie, 33.
Weishampel, David B., 25.
Weissman, Paul, 8.
Wells, Robert E., 16.
Weston, Martha, 20.
Westray, Kathleen, 16.
Wexler, Jerome, 37.

White, Laurence B., 5.
Whitfield, Philip, 21, 25.
Wiese, Jim, 16.
Wiggers, Raymond, 21, 38.
Wilkes, Angela, 5, 25.
Winner, Cherie, 58.
Wolkomir, Joyce Rogers, 48.
Wolkomir, Richard, 48.
Wollard, Kathy, 5.
Wood, A.J., 33.
Wright, Joan Richards, 57.
Wu, Norbert, 33.
Yolen, Jane, 33.
Young, Jerry, 69.
Zoehfeld, Kathleen Weidner, 33.
Zubrowski, Bernie, 16.

Title Index

Text designed by Marcia Lange and Ben Segedin
Cover designed by Marcia Lange

Text printed on 50 lb Finch Opaque White
and bound in 10-point cover stock
by IPC Publishing Services